TRUE AWAKENING

*The Highs, the Lows, and
the Mess of Spiritual Transformation*

KERRA BECKER ENGLISH

ORBIS
Maryknoll, New York 10545

Founded in 1970, Orbis Books endeavors to publish works that enlighten the mind, nourish the spirit, and challenge the conscience. The publishing arm of the Maryknoll Fathers and Brothers, Orbis seeks to explore the global dimensions of the Christian faith and mission, to invite dialogue with diverse cultures and religious traditions, and to serve the cause of reconciliation and peace. The books published reflect the views of their authors and do not represent the official position of the Maryknoll Society. To learn more about Maryknoll and Orbis Books, please visit our website at www.orbisbooks.com.

Copyright © 2025 by Kerra Becker English

Published by Orbis Books, Box 302, Maryknoll, NY 10545-0302.

Scripture quotations are from the New Revised Standard Version Bible, copyright © 1989 National Council of the Churches of Christ in the United States of America. Used by permission. All rights reserved worldwide.

All rights reserved.

This book is intended for informational and educational purposes only. The content is not meant to substitute for professional medical, psychological, or therapeutic advice, diagnosis, or treatment. Always seek the advice of qualified healthcare providers or mental health professionals regarding any questions about your personal circumstances.

Queries regarding rights and permissions should be addressed to: Orbis Books, P.O. Box 302, Maryknoll, NY 10545-0302.

Manufactured in the United States of America

Library of Congress Cataloging-in-Publication Data

Names: English, Kerra Becker, author.
Title: True awakening : the highs, the lows, and the mess of spiritual transformation / Kerra Becker English.
Description: Maryknoll, NY : Orbis Books, [2025] | Includes bibliographical references. | Summary: "Identifies the numerous ways through which inner spiritual awakening happens"— Provided by publisher.
Identifiers: LCCN 2024060245 (print) | LCCN 2024060246 (ebook) | ISBN 9781626986022 (trade paperback) | ISBN 9798888660577 (epub)
Subjects: LCSH: Spiritual life. | Spiritual formation. | Self-realization—Religious aspects.
Classification: LCC BL624 .E54 2025 (print) | LCC BL624 (ebook) | DDC 204/.4—dc23/eng/20250113
LC record available at https://lccn.loc.gov/2024060245
LC ebook record available at https://lccn.loc.gov/2024060246

To the awakening of Spirit

May it come to us

May it flow through us

CONTENTS

Foreword by Carl McColman   vii

1. Wake Up:
   The Spiritual Journey Starts Now   1

2. Get Curious:
   The Spiritual Gift with a Warning Label   16

3. Get Going:
   Great Quests Come from Great Questions   38

4. Pick a Lane:
   Choosing My Religion   58

5. Tear It All Apart:
   Losing My Religion   86

6. Survive the Dark Forest:
   Suffering Is a Feature, Not a Flaw   108

7. Let It Go:
   Unraveling the Known, Discovering Mystery   128

8. Answer the Call:
   Waking Up Every Day   152

9. Embrace the Strange and Brace for Boring:
   Meeting the Wonders and Living the Mundane   175

10. Begin Again:
    Turning with the Cycle of Life   200

Sources   227

Acknowledgments   233

FOREWORD

Carl McColman

ON DECEMBER 6, 1273, Thomas Aquinas, a Dominican friar widely regarded as one of the greatest philosophers of medieval Europe, found his life turned upside down by an unexpected mystical experience. During the Mass for the feast of Saint Nicholas, Thomas went into an ecstatic state that moved him so deeply that when he met with his close friend, Reginald, later that day, he announced that he could not finish the book he was writing. When Reginald pressed Thomas as to why he wanted to abandon his work, the friar simply said, "Mihi videtur ut palea"—"it seems like straw to me." Whatever happened to Thomas Aquinas in that moment of mystical ecstasy, it left him convinced that even the most sublime philosophy was, by comparison, worthless.

Almost a century later, in May 1373, a woman in the town of Norwich, England, fell ill—so sick that her priest was summoned to administer her last rites. As it turned out, she didn't die, but before she got better she received her own spiritual transformation: a series of mystical visions, of God and Jesus and Mary and heaven, filled with insights that gave her an entirely new perspective on her faith. Above all, her visions left her with an unshakable sense that God's love for humanity is vast, unconditional, and filled with joy. Moved by this extraordinary experience, this woman entered a life of prayer and solitude in a small cell adjacent to the Church of St. Julian. And there, she wrote a book—to the best of our knowledge, the first book written in English by a woman. Her name has been lost in the mists of time, but she became known by the name of her church and her town: Julian of Norwich.

Lest you think these kinds of gee-whiz mystical experiences only happened to saints and visionaries in the Middle Ages, here's one more for you, from the twentieth century. A British girl named Caryll Houselander had a childhood marked by illness, a broken home, and financial instability, eventually landing her in a convent school where one day she had a vision of one of the nuns wearing Jesus's crown of thorns. Not long after that came an even more dramatic vision of the spirit of Christ inhabiting every single person she saw on an ordinary day riding on the London Underground. Caryll was so moved by those events that she went on to become a best-selling writer of religious and inspirational literature in mid-twentieth-century England. All of her books and essays revolved around one central theme: the spirit of

Christ exists in the heart of every human being, and if we could truly see this, it would revolutionize our society.

The stories of Thomas Aquinas, Julian of Norwich, and Caryll Houselander are quite dramatic, so I feel I should point out (and as you'll see in this book, Kerra English agrees on this) that a spiritual awakening does not have to be "mystical" or extraordinary in order to be real: in fact, probably for most of us mere mortals, the most meaningful awakenings happen in very down-to-earth ways. But when the big ones do happen (like Paul on the road to Damascus, or Moses and the burning bush, or the enlightenment of the Buddha), they tend to get written about and documented for posterity's sake, so those are the ones we tend to reflect on years or centuries later. And so looking at the three awakenings I've shared with you, we see something remarkable: every time someone receives a spiritual awakening, their lives are transformed. A renowned philosopher lays down his pen, humbled by what he has seen. A hundred years later, an anonymous woman picks up *her* pen, finding her voice in an age when women did not write at all. Her book became the first known work written by a woman in the English language. And centuries after that, another woman's spiritual vision inspires her to write beautiful words that celebrate the power of the Spirit found within.

Yet a spiritual awakening is more than just a remarkable experience: it's an initiation, a deep and from-the-inside-out transformation that makes life irreversibly new for the one who has woken up. Think of "Rejoice," that old song by U2 where Bono sings, "I can't change the world, but I can change the world in me." The joke, of course, is that when we change the world in us, that impacts the world at large as well. Once we have a spiritual awakening, we'll never be the same—and that can make a big difference not only in your life and mine, but in ways beyond our understanding that we may never fully comprehend. After all, when Thomas Aquinas decided all his previous work was straw, could he have imagined me, on another continent some 750 years later, reflecting on what we can learn from his experience? Of course not. But consider what that means: you and I simply cannot imagine what kind of repercussions *our* awakenings might have, whether in big or small ways, over the months, years, or decades to come. Such spiritual experiences are invitations to say yes to what our awakening calls us to do. They are not just singular moments in time, but ongoing insights that change us.

Like Thomas and Julian and Caryll, Jesus of Nazareth no doubt had his own radical awakening, although the Bible really doesn't shed much light on Jesus's inner life. We just get to see the actions Jesus takes as a result: he travels for three years around Palestine, teaching and healing and inspiring people from all walks of life. When he taught, Jesus liked to ask questions: "Who do you say that I am?" "Why do you worry?" And my personal favorite, a blunt query posed to a blind man he met on the road outside of Jericho: "What do you want?" Naturally, the individual expressed his overriding need: "I want to see." But I can't help but think that he's meant to be a proxy for all human beings, including you and me. We are all blind, and we want to see. Or like the woman at the well, we are all thirsty, and we seek refreshing waters. Or like Lazarus: we are all "dead," and we crave new life.

In other words: we are all asleep, and we want to wake up.

And this brings me to someone who writes so well about awakenings and how we live them out: Kerra English. Both Kerra and I are spiritual directors, which is to say, people who accompany others on their journey into a deepening life of prayer, meditation, and intimacy with the divine. Spiritual direction, which has its roots in the early experience of monks and nuns living in the deserts of Egypt and Palestine, is a beautiful and gentle experience of exploring one's inner life through the attentive and caring presence of a prayerful companion. It's not therapy or mentoring or life coaching, nor is it like having a guru or a shaman or some sort of religious authority figure. Not all spiritual directors are Christian, but in Christian terminology we like to say that the true "director" of your soul is the indwelling spirit. Probably the most helpful metaphor for a spiritual director is a midwife: someone who offers gentle guidance and trustworthy expertise, but who simply attends to the mother who, herself, does the actual labor of giving birth. A spiritual director is a midwife for the birth of—you guessed it—an awakened soul.

The journey of giving birth to the transformed world that can emerge only out of our hearts is the same journey that Caryll Houselander writes about in her most famous book, *The Reed of God*. Everyone who follows the way of Jesus, she suggests, is invited to be like Mary, the mother of Jesus, to "give birth" to Jesus in their own life. Even for those who don't identify as Christians, this still holds, just in a broader sense: for no matter what spiritual or religious label we do (or don't) wear, we all are called to give birth to love, to compassion, to justice, to peace, to reconciliation. But just as a midwife cannot do the work of giving birth for the mother, no one can replace us on our own awakening journey.

In this book, Kerra tells her own story of spiritual awakenings (yes, plural: I imagine most people get "awakened" multiple times over the course of their lives); and she also draws from the wisdom and insight of other great awakeners like Julian of Norwich or Teresa of Ávila, the passionate Spanish Carmelite nun who wrote mystical masterpieces like *The Interior Castle*. One of the occupational hazards of writing about spiritual experience is that we writers sometimes make it all sound too neat, clean, and orderly—which can make it sound like spiritual growth follows a tidy and predictable pattern from Point A (for Awakening) to Point E (for Enlightenment).

Thankfully, Kerra does a splendid job at reminding us that spiritual awakenings actually tend to be quirky, messy, and sometimes even just plain weird. They can be subtle, so Kerra helps us to recognize them when they show up. They can sometimes seem unsettling or even threatening, so we might need the reassurance of a friend or the support of a community. They can be mysterious, so sometimes we have to take time to really understand what's happening to us. And so on, depending on the layers within our experiences.

Yet whatever transformation we happen to find ourselves in, this book helps us recognize our one-of-a-kind spiritual process, and learn to meet our souls. There's no cut-and-dried formula for this: in fact, spiritual directors quickly learn that everyone's inner journey is unique and unrepeatable. You are a limited edition of one, just like everyone else. Therefore, your spiritual transformation is yours and yours alone.

No book can give you the formula for your awakening —and *True Awakening* is among the very few writings on spiritual transformation that acknowledges this fact. That's why this book is so valuable—as even so, it still *can* give you plenty of inspiration and insight into the lay of the land, as it beckons you to walk the path that exists only for you.

Kerra English is humble enough to refuse to pass herself off as a spiritual master, but she is wise enough to truly be a trusted friend. And like a friend at a sleepover, when she shakes your shoulder and whispers in your ear, "It's time to wake up!" do pay attention to her. Like all good companions, she would only do that because there's something truly worth waking up for.

1

WAKE UP
The Spiritual Journey Starts Now

Shit helps things grow, love.
　　　　　　　　　　—Mae, in *Ted Lasso*

Ecstasy is not fun.
　　　　　　　　　　—Huston Smith

AWAKENINGS SUCK. They just do. Spiritual awakenings can feel a lot like mental breakdowns, depression, grief, rage, or just plain losing it. Fifteenth-century mystic Teresa of Ávila describes her deepest spiritual moments as being accompanied by seemingly unending copious tears. Brene Brown's viral TED talk on vulnerability includes a slide with the words "Spiritual Awakening" crossed out and the word "Breakdown" underneath describing her own journey studying human emotion.

Mystics walk a lonely path. Prophets are considered fools. The spiritual giants of just about every religious tradition are known for the trials they endured. The transformative dark night of the soul isn't exactly sunshine and rainbows. And even in times when spiritual growth is of the less dramatic variety, it is frequently associated with loss—loss of innocence, loss of confidence, loss of certainty in something we once thought to be unquestionable, or loss of identity itself.

Yes, awakenings may be accompanied by the joy that comes with the morning, but this book is written for those of us who are in the "Don't bother me until I've had at least one cup of coffee" crowd. Certainly, within these pages, I also describe wondrous moments of being awestruck, and I hope to look together at what it's like to fall crazy in love with the spiritual life—but the reality persists that the work of transformation is complicated and frequently accompanied by rough patches along the way for the person being transformed.

If you are looking for the easy alternative, when the Spirit comes to tap you on your shoulder, just pull the covers over your head and stay asleep. Many do exactly that by denying that change is even possible or by numbing the incessant, nagging inner voice that intuits that your life could be different.

But if you want to be fully awake to spiritual reality and guided by the truth, buckle up. It will take courage. (Even after your first cup of coffee.) Inevitably, you will feel not only your own pain but the pain of others, and you will find yourself identifying with the suffering of this world. Fun, right?

It hurts when we realize that our human systems do not bend toward justice nearly as much as we would like, and that those on top in wealth, status, or power gain from exalting themselves and punishing those who strive for the good of all. Systems of oppression work exactly as they are designed to work. They benefit when those who might wake up to empathy for their fellow human beings are too afraid to make waves or too tired to care. Those who are walking the spiritual path can't help but notice the reality of those who are suffering under the weight of the world. Those who act with a heart for solidarity are doing hard soul work. Once your eyes have been opened to the prophetic understanding that the world, as it is, isn't all that it could be, it's tough to shove that knowledge back into the box from whence it came.

So, by waking up, you become one of those people who gives a damn about the world. Good job! The world needs more people invested in this life beyond their own selfish interests. Moving from me to we opens you up to experiencing sleepless nights and a heaping dose of crippling anxiety seemingly absent in the more narcissistic among us. This existential angst that reminds you that all is *not* well may disturb you, but the disruption may just guide you toward healing and growth, which are the fruit to be gained from all this challenging work.

As difficult as they are, awakenings are the fertilizer of personal growth. The basic premise for individual spiritual growth and understanding is so simple as to seem stupid: Get curious about knowing yourself. That's it, the starting point. And even though studying the teachings of philosophical traditions and religious practices can be helpful, and examining the revelations that come from experience can be interesting, it's still all about doing the interior work that allows us to understand authentically who we are. No one can make you do it. No one else can do it for you. You hold the keys. You can embrace the spiritual path and start to get comfortable with the inevitable changes that will happen to you when you follow it.

Alternatively, you can either fight it or say eff-it when the allure wears off because it either got too hard or very boring. There's no shame in coming back into the comfort of regular old human existence until the next turn calls you back. And it will.

No matter what anyone says or how some religious traditions offer you clear steps, there are no GPS coordinates. There's no clear signage. There's no one right way to follow the spiritual journey. It is a meandering path, not a straightforward one. And trust me on this, you will not ever, in your whole lifetime, exhaust the possibilities for knowing more about who you are and who you are becoming in this world. Can't be done. I don't care how spiritually amazing you happen to be. The fun never ends. Keep on seeking a more authentic version of yourself in service of God and the world, and you will be blessed by the work—as hard as it might be. Then you will start all over again. Ha!

Just when you think you have reached some amazing level of nirvana, full enlightenment, exquisite oneness with the Christ, out of nowhere will appear something or someone who will take you down a notch. You will have a day when you feel like starting completely over because your fumbling self feels like it has garnered no accumulated wisdom whatsoever. But then, on other days, when your heart is open, a moment will startle and surprise you. You will be so taken aback by the circumstances of your own life that you will recognize and be glad for the new person you have become. When you begin to adjust your eyes to the possibility of waking up—of seeing reality as it truly is, with all the beauty and the tragedy mingled together—then in all stages of your life you might notice awakenings that are both remarkably profound and wonderfully ordinary.

My hope in sharing my thoughts about this journey as someone who is a spiritual director and guide is that in identifying the common threads of what differentiates spiritual awakening from, well, everything else, there's insight for your own journey. Spiritual transformation can be confused with other life experiences that also suck, like depression, grief, anger, and the like. But most certainly a person can experience great hardship or trauma without it ever being transformative or understood as some sort of spiritual gift. We don't need to tell ourselves or others in pain that God is testing us or giving it to them for a reason. That's a shitty move. The difference is subtle, but I don't want any confusion. Though I may make the claim that awakenings suck, not everything that sucks is an awakening. And just because you fell on your face doesn't mean you are receiving a message from God that you are going in the wrong direction. It may simply mean that you tripped over a crack in the sidewalk. Got it?

Spiritual awakening can also be confused with the mask of religious intensity. Maybe you meet someone who is white-hot with the fire of their faith, and they act as though they possess accurate knowledge on every opinion that God and the whole universe have about right and wrong. And perhaps you are not so sure. Here's what's going on. The fundamentalists and zealots of every, and I mean *every*, religious conviction would love to tell you exactly what the correct spiritual path is and why you aren't on it. There is power associated with being certain of your own beliefs, and some presume that power is the same thing as having spiritual acumen. Those who are convinced they are right might also presume that they are the most awakened person in the room. But the true spiritually curious person is more likely to be the one flooded by doubts and uncertainty. They know what they don't know, and they know that it's *a lot*.

So, if you are inclined to strut your spiritual stuff and dismiss others for being less enlightened than you are, then there's likely a pedestal just waiting to be kicked out from under you. The moment of awakening does not come from reaching a quota of people you have bullied into your own point of view. The moment of awakening is when you let that pedestal fall, giving you the opportunity to learn new things by experiencing a few passing moments on your ass.

And if you are someone who has rejected the path of spiritual awakening just because you have met some folks who walk around as though they wear a halo they know you just can't see, please don't let this deter you. The assholes who pretentiously try to hide their assholery under the cover of religion disguised as spiritual know-it-alls are still, at the end of the day, just a-holes awaiting spiritual awakening, unbeknownst to them.

Religious practices, traditions, and concepts will have an important place in this book as we look at the highs and lows of spiritual awakenings. This shouldn't be a surprise. And we'll look at terms, like *religion*, to start—which, loosely defined, is about believing in a divine power or being greater than oneself, where it is presumed by many that the source of such power inspires spiritual illumination by way of holy interventions. At the same time, it is also true that many hateful things have been done under the auspices of maintaining the purity of a particular religious expression. Religious genocide, condemnation of those deemed too sinful to be part of the tradition, holy wars, the inquisition, execution of heretics, and the like remind us that those who claim belief in God are not necessarily moved to compassion, something I think happens in conjunction with the spiritual awakening process. But when you can put your trust in the possibility of divinely inspired connections, either within an established religious tradition or with your own sense of a power greater than you alone, I believe you will get to know yourself in a fuller, more spiritually attuned way. And as you come to a greater understanding of yourself, you will find a stronger connection with others regardless of your or their religious affiliation.

Religions, in the cultural sense, that have a shared belief system about God and a history that has established them as a known unit, organization, or entity are neither all good nor all bad. I'm not here to defend them or fight against them. It is not my job, at least not in this book, to say if Christianity is a good or an evil in this era or any other. Rather, I view Christianity (and other world religions) as a practice, or a methodology toward the understanding of God. Though religion may lend us a vocabulary for describing God, religion ultimately isn't that which it describes. The power greater than we are eludes being confined by any box we create to contain it.

But it's important, by way of self-introduction, to also say that Christianity is my chosen religion, not because I think it is superior to other religious traditions, rather because it grew to be my personal foundation. I was baptized and brought up in a small Presbyterian congregation in rural West Virginia, and I've stuck with the tradition I started with even though I've had my share of contentious disagreements with institutional Christianity of just about every variety. My greatest hope for this communal aspect of my spiritual life is that I love my tradition enough to be challenged by it, but that I won't love it too much and so cease to wrestle with its downsides.

Reader and spiritual pilgrim, companions on this journey, as you are contemplating the ideas in this book or trying some of the suggestions in it, if any of the ways I render my god-language isn't particularly compelling for you—feel free to adapt it in a meaningful way. This author won't mind. So if, for instance, I talk about Christ, and you are a Buddhist—allow the spirit with which I am expressing my truth to help you see connections to your truth. No name-brand religion has a trademark that can be put on these musings about spirituality. And it hurts my ego a little bit to tell you this, but you won't discover anything new written here. That's the hope of just about every writer, right? That you will say the thing that hasn't been said before. The best I can hope to do is put a spin on some very old truths so they can be heard by those who long for someone to really see them on the journey toward spiritual awareness. I see you. Others see you. The Divine sees you.

Spiritual awakening is not new, but neither is it a concept that is frequently discussed either in circles of the Christian faithful, or in the realm of the more-secular-than-spiritual-but-still-curious. I would love to see that change! I borrow the word *awakening* from Buddhism because equivalent language has all but been erased from contemporary Christianity. It turns out that awakenings aren't well suited to institutional preservation, and these days, as participation in organized religion wanes, self-awareness and spiritual acuity can be viewed as threats to keeping the bureaucracy afloat. That rising number of "nones" (those with no identified religious affiliation per survey questionnaires) scares the bejesus out of religious folk, not because they can't see the point, but because it means that the money religion made by having butts in pews might drift elsewhere.

All that said, religious practices *are* woven all through the process of spiritual awakening, even as they are not the same thing. The directness of a spiritual encounter may be a cause for deepening connection to your chosen religion, or it may be a reason for changing or abandoning it. Religious voices become problematic when they demand adherence and shout for exclusive attention to their rules without exception—including dismissing spiritual encounters that don't fit their mold. Religious community befriends and encourages connections with the holy when genuine spiritual experience is welcomed, discussed, and encouraged. The danger has always been present in every religious expression that it will become a replacement for God by hanging on to an ideology so tightly and so inflexibly that there's no room for the spirit to breathe anew. And yet prayer, studying holy texts, meditation, and ritual all are windows that let the air in. Truly they are. It is telling that such practices have stuck with us for damn near close to the whole of human existence. I'd hate to see us throw out the wisdom that all the various expressions of world religions have to offer just because spirituality is the more popular kid on the block right now. What I am interested in is discovering how we come to develop a deeper understanding of ourselves so that we can nurture the kind of wisdom that leads us to a connectedness we can feel with the Divine, the universe, and ultimately each other.

In a time like our own—of geopolitical realignments, economic uncertainty, and fragile ecosystems—there is also the possibility of spiritual transformation such that we will emerge with creativity and hopeful possibilities on the other side of this adventure. We need the melancholy mystics and pissed-off prophets who are willing and able to carry the heavy burden of self-awareness. Lest we think that self-awareness is something like self-improvement where our paychecks and our ability to effect change grow bigger with each step up and forward, self-awareness can be more like a downward spiral, taking us on a deep exploration of our own limitations and mortality.

The spiritual path is not linear. If you expect it in your own life to follow the outline of this book exactly, you will be quickly disappointed. Yet there *is* common ground to share—spiritual understandings that human beings have been experiencing and seeking to describe for millennia. As a starting point, it's helpful to note that generally, in the first half of life, spirituality is about exploration, wonder, and belonging—and in the second half of life, spirituality is about depth, mystery, and compassion. These halves are not set by any one calendar though. Life experience takes us on this journey, and different people adapt differently along the way. A person can be curious their whole life and find joy in simply living out of the beauty of creation, or a person can experience hardship at a young age and develop a wise understanding of suffering before turning twenty-one. Unlike religion, where there is a defined history, cultural adaptation, and frequently guiding texts, here, there are no rules, just lived experience.

Even to attempt to describe what makes an awakening true and how it might become the impetus for spiritual transformation is something I do through the sharing of common insights I've gathered. I hope the insights will prove helpful, a kind of guide along the way.

Identifying an awakening moment can be profoundly personal, yet I don't think that it's so obscure as to be indescribable. As I see it, an awakening is an event or experience that offers you an awareness about yourself, your environment, or your spiritual life that you didn't have before. For it to be discerned as *true,* it must line up with a broader sense of love, mercy, grace, and justice—the humanitarian values found at the core of every major world religion. A true awakening has some aspect of being "for" the benevolence of others, not just yourself. If you find a lottery ticket and assume God wants you to be a billionaire, that might not mean what you think it means. Just sayin'. And finally, deep in my heart, I know that this up-and-down, confusing, complex, messy journey of awakening *is* the direct path to spiritual transformation. The awakening gives you an awareness, the awareness opens you to the love of God, and the love of God changes hearts and minds. Every single moment of every single day. This isn't only the journey of messiahs and prophets. It is your journey too.

Awakened people will be the ones who awaken more people. Which parts of this book resonate may matter less than how the book complements your own personal desire to seek greater knowledge of who you are and why you are here. As Joseph Campbell so aptly said, "We must let go of the life we have planned so as to accept the one that is waiting for us." Letting go will be an ongoing part of this process of noticing our awakenings. But when we meet those who are on that same path, who have sensed the spark of the Divine within them, we will want to listen to their stories, learn from their wisdom, and emulate the lives they are living. Margaret Mead, the American cultural anthropologist, suggested that ultimately it will be small groups of dedicated people who will change the world. And I agree with her researched conclusion. It's the only thing that ever has.

So, buckle up for the ride, this roller coaster is going somewhere!

TIME TO WAKE UP

Each chapter of this book offers you moments of engagement to assist you on your personal awakening journey—questions to think about. Ideas to ponder. If you were wondering when, the answer is now. If you were wondering how, I hope you'll find some tips on how to pay attention. If you were wondering why, it's because awakened people awaken other people (and I think we should start a trend!). It's as hard and as easy as that.

Waking up is hard to do.

It means change. It means eyes wide open to the truth. It means potential heartbreak over the pain of the world. It may mean feeling small in your attempts to make a change.

Where in your life are you encountering a nudge for change?

Pay close attention to the change that comes from your inner being. It could be an awakening moment.

Waking up can become a part of your routine.

If you know what conditions could help you wake up, like setting your morning alarm, you will be ready to encounter an awakening when it sets off bells you recognize.

How is your routine supporting the life you want to live?
What changes might you make to embrace that life?

Waking up is easy when the day is glorious!

The beauty of the world is staggering—if you pause to notice it. Awe and wonder can be found in both the simplest and most complex moments of life itself. Such overwhelming love for what is—and what is right in front of you—is the chef's kiss of awakening.

Watch a sunset. Go sit by the body of water closest to you. Observe the wild animals in your neighborhood. Allow the world to show you its beauty. I promise you won't be disappointed.

2

GET CURIOUS
The Spiritual Gift with a Warning Label

The important thing is not to stop questioning.
Curiosity has its own reason for existing.

—Albert Einstein

"Where was I before I was born?" I once asked my mother when I was very young. She thought I wanted to know where babies come from and tried to answer accordingly. But I brushed her off. NO! I insisted. Before I was a baby. Before you were pregnant. You know. *Before.*

For that, she had no answer.

From that point forward, perhaps at times to my mother's dismay, I made a lifelong habit of asking questions and seeking knowledge.

Human beings are observably curious from early childhood, but often we grow away from it to be quite cautious. Yet I believe curiosity is our most underutilized spiritual gift, perhaps a gift we avoid as it always arrives with a warning label attached. Whether we are the openers of Pandora's box or, like Eve, the consumers of forbidden fruit, curiosity opens us to the peril of risk. You won't find one without the other.

The Jewish and Christian traditions share an origin story centering curiosity as the very reason human beings are the way they are. In the beginning God creates all the things that allow life to flourish, including humans. God then sets these humans, Adam and Eve, in a lush garden with two specific trees in it—the tree of life and the tree of the knowledge of good and evil. Supposedly, if they eat from the tree of knowledge, they will die. Warning label aside, it doesn't take much convincing for them to get curious about it. They develop such a strong desire to obtain knowledge for themselves that they take a bite from its fruit, and it turns around and bites them in the ass.

Surprisingly, given the specificity of the cautionary language, the two did not drop dead. What happens next is quite interesting: They have an awakening. What do they see? They see themselves. They recognize their vulnerability. They are naked. They are alone. They feel their separation from each other. They are spiritually cut off from the garden paradise. They now know that they can eff things up and be a disappointment both to one another and to God. Turns out that knowing the difference between good and evil opens the door to sin, but it also opens the door to accountability. It won't take long in this religious narrative for humankind to start asking just how responsible they are for the well-being of others. After the first fratricide, their murderous son will be the one to ask the question, "What am I? My brother's keeper?" Turns out awakening isn't an end in itself. It asks something of us. And suddenly we meet a set of stories of awakening where individuals make a quick leap from self-awareness to making excuses for our behavior.

Curious folk have often speculated as to what life was like *before* "the fall of humankind," which means *before* this human awakening. It's not that dissimilar from the sentiment behind my childhood question. Where would we be without self-awareness? Before we were born. Perhaps it is bliss. Perhaps it is nothingness. Perhaps it is exceedingly boring and one would rather risk death than remain in such an unfulfilled stupor.

Before you think that I'm taking this biblical story as literal truth rather than as a story seeking to describe the indescribable phenomenon of human self-awareness, recall that in our own time neuroscience is also asking its own questions about the nature of human consciousness. Scientists study brain activity, cognitive understanding, and human behavior, and then they theorize about this awareness we know as intimately as our own minds, and yet the human experience still isn't yielding its mysteries to clear explanations. Where today we might interview subjects through longitudinal studies or observe brain waves in MRI machines, the ancients wrote stories to try to explain what they were seeing in their own time.

We have this curiosity about wanting to know, deeply, who we are. As a lifelong Presbyterian, one of my theological forebears John Calvin hooked me from early on with these words: "Nearly all the wisdom we possess, that is to say, true and sound wisdom, consists of two parts: the knowledge of God and of ourselves." As curmudgeonly as he is portrayed by many of his biographers, he was a knowledge-seeker not unlike the stargazer Galileo. He wrote broadly about insights he gained from Scripture, but also about the created world as if written into the rocks and trees and animals was truth to be discovered about our Creator, ourselves, and our world.

In our own time, we may not be seeking an origin story to tell us that Pandora's box of troubles is only opened through daring and curiosity or that in some traditions the first humans were curious, tempted, awakened, then cursed by eating the fruit of all-knowing-ness. But what these stories reveal that maybe we learned from going to a few therapy sessions is that increasing our level of self-awareness is painful. Getting curious enough to wake up to who we really are causes trouble and feels like a curse. Once I start asking questions about who I am, I face the vulnerability of being misunderstood, being alone, being scared, and being hurt. I also become accountable for my actions that could be interpreted as good or bad, fair or unfair, by members of my family, by my partner, or by friends and colleagues. We carry this hurt around with us, and until we start getting curious about the origins of our pain, we will continue to operate as though it is impossible to change. This is not the fun part of curiosity. It's hard. But turning toward curiosity when we are feeling low or insecure is one of the tried-and-true ways of becoming more conscious of our own power to heal ourselves and our relationships with others.

And yet those who are bold enough to be curious, those tempted to ask the deepest and hardest questions about who they are, will be rewarded with the amazing gifts that go with that risk: both knowledge of self and empathy for the other. Honoring the miraculous spark of selfhood kicks us out of the idyllic garden of ignorance, crying as we do with our first breath of life in a world of responsibility. Then we may even get curious about the expectations the Divine has for us. Why am I here? Is there a purpose to life itself? Am I, like Cain, responsible for those nasty thoughts I have when I am feeling insecure about myself and begin to compare myself to my siblings? Do I have to love my neighbor? Even *that* neighbor? Those questions peel back the layers, but they also make life far messier. Not everyone will be all that thrilled about our desire to know ourselves so completely. About the eight millionth time I asked the question *why*, my parents were ready to put that curiosity right back into the *before* where it came from.

As we answer curiosity's call to awaken and start to seek answers to those questions about who we really are and who the Divine wants us to be, we may feel the pressure of those who don't want us to grow because they fear how our growth might challenge their own choice to stay the same. Awakening tends to be contagious, and those who are most fearful will feel that they might get that "ick" of wokeness on them and then they might have to start asking "Why?" themselves. There will be pressure for you to accept whatever label you've been given, and to keep sealed the box that they've put you in, lest you escape and become more magnificent than they could imagine you to be. Though our lives have been shaped and formed by a multitude of factors that are out of our control, it is ultimately up to us to determine if those factors will launch the possibility for our growth or impose the limits that get us stuck in the status quo. The language we speak, the color of our skin, the communities that surround us, the resources available to our family, our sexual preferences, our gender, our abilities or lack thereof—the list of reasons for others to judge us is rather endless. When the risk of embracing our own uniqueness puts us outside the norms others have set for us, or expect of us, we might adapt to the pressure by being just a little less curious and a little more cautious. Trying to figure out good from bad, fair from unfair, truth from assumptions and speculations, we stifle curiosity to do what it takes to feel the approval of others and fit in.

Spiritual curiosity moves us. It can take us back to our childhood curiosity, to a time when we were able to be amazed by the simplest pleasures. We reexperience that ease and tranquility falling into the arms of a loved one or smelling the freshness of a cascading waterfall. Such awe allows us to put our trust in the goodness of our Creator. Curiosity can also take us forward when we welcome it into the complexities of life, giving us the courage to wonder how it could all be "more." Why, we ask, *wouldn't* we want to know ourselves better? We have questions. We wonder. We want to know about ourselves and our place in this beautiful world, and that search turns us to questions about the mysteries of life and the Divine in the grandest sense. It's an example of what the meditation practitioners call "beginner's mind." We set aside all those assumptions of what we are "supposed" to be, laid on us by family and friends, and we begin fresh, allowing the environment and our internal landscapes to speak to us through all the clutter.

Though I would call curiosity an innate gift that begins as exploration and play in children, curiosity as a lifelong pursuit is the creative spark for innovators, the serenity of the mystics, the passion of the prophets, and the joy of the enlightened. Almost no growth or learning happens without it—at least not the sustainable kind.

Returning repeatedly to a curious mind is the basis of spiritual growth. Every "aha" moment is an opportunity for awakening. Maybe every "oh no" moment too. Remember that awakening is simply being able to sustain an awareness that you didn't have before about yourself, your environment, or your spiritual life.

Once you are awakened to even a tiny detail in a new way, then you have a legitimate choice about what to do with that tiny thing and how best to incorporate that knowing into how you live your life. Will you move forward transformed? Will you want to slip back into the convenience of not knowing? Will you brush this new information off as unimportant? Or will it reorient your life completely?

That's why awakening is so horribly frightening for the not-so-curious. From parents who want to keep children safe, to whole systems that work to keep social and economic hierarchies in place, the desire to limit the choices of others, even of others we care about, is significant. Sometimes we would rather that folks have no choice than to allow all the possibilities that arise out of curiosity.

How marvelously *dangerous* to the status quo is acknowledging curiosity as a spiritual gift. The drive to sameness assures that any novel or revolutionary thought stays deeply buried, even if it means burying spiritual gold with it. I can practically guarantee that your local faith community would just rather you didn't wonder about

God too much, or at least not wonder about what they were telling you about God so much. Right? Awakening is dangerous.

Yet spiritual curiosity yields supremely personal insights about human life and our relationship with the Divine. Those insights cannot be trademarked and owned by any one religion or truth. Our open inquiries may affirm the truth within religious understanding, or they may expose the bullshit of religious propaganda.

What I want you to know, which I haven't always been sure of myself, is that your personal experience matters—and the choices that you make matter. I was taught that the ultimate scandal of becoming a spiritual guide is making the affirmation that each unique individual, each *Self*, has their own spiritual journey to follow. What you are curious about will lead you to your awakening. You can't get that part wrong. The choices that you make will have consequences, and navigating those consequences can help you on the road to transformation. If curiosity is your guide, then your life choices build the path you are walking.

In this book I share stories of my own seeking and awakening and stories of others so that maybe you'll recognize something familiar, something that resonates with the curiosity that you have noticed in yourself. We'll look at common patterns, because while your journey is special, it doesn't make you more special than anyone else who is on their own path. It's both wonderful and humbling to notice that you are now connecting with the very depths of the Divine even as it may feel crappy to think that the jerk next to you could be meandering their way to the very same truth. Part of what is troubling about awakening is that taking the interior journey will remind you of how insignificant you are or how little you've grown, or what little influence you have on this very large and mysterious world. But there are ways to tell if your personal awakening coincides with broader patterns of awakening that are the means of spiritual transformation.

When our journey aligns with the divine path, it leads to some awesome outcomes for humanity in general. We might feel humbled and small. But we also start to see how we connect to something so vast that we discover a different type of meaning. From curiosity comes four (as I see it) results that will always make a difference—that when combined offer healing not only personally but globally. When curiosity is leading us to awakening, there are signs that help us determine if awakening actually is what it seems to be. In ourselves or others or even movements, we can discern if we are on the path to spiritual transformation by looking for these results: feeling at home in the natural world, intuiting a sense of belonging to the human family, amplifying the goals of justice and right-relationship, and cultivating hope instead of fear.

Feeling at Home in the World

It's no surprise that nature arouses the curiosity of the human animal. Watching beautiful sunsets, powerful rainstorms, waterfalls, and wild animals connects us to beauty and inspiration and lets us know that we are part of the natural world.

Just think about the distance between our planet and the sun, or the sun and the next closest star we can see—it is mind-blowing to contemplate the vastness of our universe—and our place in it. Or go another direction and imagine the activity of microcosm, the atomic, or subatomic level. Consider the specificity of the conditions that lead to the possibility of life itself. Curiosity introduces us to her sister: wonder.

Curiosity nudges us to make observations and ask questions. When it becomes clear that the world is an amazing place, and we find ourselves comforted and amazed by being part of it—then we experience wonder. Awe. A moment that shuts us up and allows us to simply be.

For me, when I was a kid, the place I went to nurture this communion with nature was a treehouse my dad built in our yard. I would spend hours there, sometimes reading, sometimes just thinking, always happy to be outside. If I was out closer to twilight, I could watch the sun dipping behind the mountains and occasionally see a grazing deer or watch a fox dart through to the underbrush behind the house. Sure, there were also roaming dogs and cats at the time (no leash laws in my rural neighborhood!). It was a place of wonder that invited me anytime. I didn't need to wait for friends to come out to ride their bikes or play ball. I could be there alone—for hours.

Maybe that was an early sign of my comfort with solitude. Maybe that was what made me contemplative.

I never outgrew my wonder for the natural world. Even as I have moved into cities or suburbs, I look for the trees, the water, the spring toads, the flowers in the sidewalk cracks. Like naturalist John Muir I prefer the saunter to the hike. When in nature, I want to slow down and take my time observing every smooth rock and smelling the dampness of the forest floor. It is renewing to my core. And yet, when I ponder the disconnect between the drive to produce and consume in my day-to-day world and compare that to the ease of being and flourishing that comes from a few hours in the forest, my curiosity nudges me toward giving a damn about taking from the creation that always seems to be giving toward me. My curiosity again inspires a shift in consciousness from thinking about the earth as a resource to being reminded that the earth is a living biome that may be affected by my own life choices.

However, not everyone lets their curiosity change their perception. Back when I was in seminary, I took a course from a Bible professor who scoffed at what she called "nature religion." She got irritated if anyone talked about knowledge of God that didn't come from the Bible itself. She thought that feeling awe at watching a sunrise or noticing the divine handprint in the ordering of the stars smacked of the time of the goddesses. Maybe it does. Her rabid scholarliness of studying the Bible with such a singular focus seemed rather patriarchal to me. So maybe now is the perfect time for a renewal of the time of goddesses, or a reconnection with the peoples of the earth who had a much better and more sacred relationship with the natural world. If we tap back into the gardens of our origins and imagine we have been set in this world in curiosity and awe and to care for this planet we call home, we will need to wake up to the ways we are connected to nature, how we are a part of it, and how we depend on its beauty and abundance for our own species to thrive.

TIME TO WAKE UP

Wonder

Ponder your own curiosity about the natural world. Where do you feel "at home" in nature? Do you pause for such moments to let them sink in while you are experiencing them? When was the last time you literally sunk your hands into the dirt, or sniffed the air with the same intensity as a hound seeking information from the breeze? Do you use your senses to engage in the present moment? How does the sun or the rain feel on your face? Take that experience to awaken your connection to the broader world. Do you feel small and insignificant standing by the ocean? Does life feel big and amazingly interconnected as you watch bees pollinate flowers? Does the complexity of it all remind you of how little you know, and then shatter your own sense of importance in the world? Good! Then take that mess brought on by your experience and broaden it to how you might act in the world. Do consuming and receiving feel different spiritually? What has the forest, beach, or desert taught you?

Intuiting a Sense of Belonging to the Human Family

If what we observe in nature shows us our place in the natural world, then what we observe from being human helps us understand ourselves in relationship with others. We learn how to read faces, how to speak a common language, how to navigate diverse relationships—from family to friendships, to lovers, to social communities. The more curious we are, the more we will comprehend how our interactions create either harmony or disconnection, because human beings yearn for a sense of belonging and community. As we put our theories into practice with our neighbors, we intuit that our interactions have consequences, whether intentional or unintentional, and we come to adjust our behaviors accordingly.

As we come to seek emotional rewards for our interconnectedness, we quickly learn if an environment is safe for our curiosity or if our curiosity will reach a limit.

Not all people will value curiosity, and that's when it gets messy as we try to determine if someone is guarding our safety or hindering our growth. When we experience what hurts us, we begin to learn what has the possibility of hurting us again. As children, some of our first lessons are that the cat might scratch. The parent might scold. The friend might leave us alone on the playground. And as children, depending upon how those around us reacted to our pain, we might have been encouraged to take more chances or discouraged from acting even the slightest bit out of the norm for fear of reprisals. What we learn early on can be so difficult to unlearn. It can be so much easier to stay stuck feeling alone and afraid than to try the alternatives. Staying curious or returning to curiosity, even when the stakes seem high, allows us to awaken to novel possibilities for rebuilding trust in work colleagues even if childhood playground experiences made you feel left out and unsupported. And being curious about the way you experienced your parents can help you have the courage to change the way you respond to your own children. The regular pain of life as it comes shapes us, no doubt. Being curious about it can transform the pain and allow us to use it for our own personal growth. This kind of curiosity looks a lot like what I would call "grace." We can take what has wounded us and allow it to become an opportunity for growth by imagining that other people have been just as hurt and frightened as we were.

That said, experiencing trauma of any type or at any time is almost guaranteed to challenge a person's ability to stay curious. To try to preserve a sense of safety in an unsafe environment is to perhaps overdevelop a sense of caution with regard to life in community. Curiosity feels dangerous, and those who have been harmed through trauma often do not where to begin. Even beginning feels beyond just messy. It can feel dangerous. Those who have experienced trauma who feel drawn to strengthen their curiosity may want to first explore curiosity with people they most feel safe with—a trusted friend, a reliable therapist, a spiritual leader, or a teacher who is kind and patient. Even voicing a desire for more curiosity and naming fear is a beginning place. If trauma has dampened your sense of curiosity, then honor the role caution has played for protection until you can tap back into your curious nature.

Finding those trusted communities where curiosity is encouraged will help you deepen your sense of belonging to the human family. Whether you have been hurt or not, whether you are shy or intrepid when it comes to diving into the questions of life, those of us who journey along the path of awakening find an inner courage that allows for exploration as well as an outer kindness that engages them with others, allowing them to see more similarity than difference in their relationships.

TIME TO WAKE UP

Balance

We've all experienced times when our curiosity was either rewarded or thwarted. Go back to those times and ask yourself what you learned. Who makes you feel like you belong? Can you share with that person how much they mean to you? Also, imagine the person who feels most unlike you: How are they a part of the same human family as you? What boundaries help you feel safe enough to be curious?

Amplifying the Goals of Justice and Right-Relationship

Those who are awakening to the spiritual path will be perceived as increasingly courageous and empathetic. Justice and righteousness will not be a prize given only to the few; they will be abundant gifts for the multitudes. The prophetic voices in every age have been my example for leading this charge to fully honoring the sacredness of all humankind. They are known for speaking truth to power and are especially good at reminding us that feeling empathy for others is a God-thing. This raw combination of boldly drawing attention to abuses of power and radically sympathizing with those on the fringes is widely thought of as a bad idea. It may get them trolled on the internet, fired from a job, or in some cases, killed for using their voice. Unfortunately, we humans are known for setting up systems of hierarchical power, being stingy with mediating justice, and counting righteousness as doing things *my way*. Having an empathetic heart within a ruthless system is a terrible mess to manage. The desire to protect that open heart from further pain is real.

The Golden Rule that shows up in so many religious traditions as a simple mandate is about such perspective taking. "Do unto others as you would have them do unto you." Can you truly imagine how you would feel in someone else's circumstances? That's a basic human skill that toddlers show signs of developing before any formal schooling begins. Quite early on we learned that if we help others, they might be likely to help us, and if we hurt others, they may return the unwanted favor of hurting us back.

Such radical empathy itself is a form of curiosity—being curious about the plight or joy of someone other than yourself. That ability to be other-focused is a profound step along the path of enlightenment. It doesn't mean you forget about the need for understanding yourself. Jesus's second commandment is to love your neighbor *as* you love yourself. It's a similar riff on the same theme. When we connect through curiosity we become open to the possibility of seeing another person's point of view, and to being helpful to them when we can.

TIME TO WAKE UP

Empathy

Reflect on the Golden Rule that is foundational in multiple religions:

- *"Do unto others as you would have them do unto you" (Christianity).*
- *"Whatever is disagreeable to yourself, do not do unto others" (Buddhism).*
- *"What is hateful to you, do not do to your fellow-man. This is the entire Law, all the rest is commentary (Judaism).*
- *"None of you will believe until you love for your brother what you love for yourself (Islam).*

Remember a time when you did exactly that: cared for a person in a way you would want to be cared for yourself. Do you find yourself to be an empathetic person? Too much? Not enough? About right? How can you be curious about cultivating this spiritual gift? Where did this first awaken in you? What opens the possibility for you to see someone as they truly are? And what about the justice side of this equation? When has your caring bolstered your courage to be honest in a place where that felt dangerous?

Cultivating Hope Instead of Fear

Glennon Doyle wrote a blessing I say to myself all the time: "Be brave, you are a child of God. Be kind, everyone else is too." Those who are awakening on the spiritual path will be living courageous, openhearted, vulnerable lives. Messy, right? I know, it sickens my stomach too to think about it. It means showing up fearless. Damn, if that isn't the hardest thing to do when the news is consistently about what sucky, dreadful policy is being proposed, or what hurtful, hateful violent event just happened.

The mystics and spiritually attuned listeners of old lived in awful times much like our own, and they also experienced a similar reality where hierarchy in religion and in other socially patriarchal systems were filled with arrogant, self-serving bastards. Priests and rulers have perpetually held pissing contests over power. The rich fill themselves with good things while the poor are emptied of the little they have that is necessary for survival. I mean, gee, how little has truly changed. It was in such a hierarchy that biblical women, like Miriam, Hannah, and Mary, the mother of Jesus, were awakened to the reality of their own situations and the challenge of hope as they raised their voices and sang intensely hopeful protest songs about switching the order of things on its head.

Centuries later, in the medieval world, Julian of Norwich committed herself to living simply, in a small walled-in space, with a cat as companion. During the great plague, people sought her out for spiritual advice, and she shared the insight of her own awakening, when she heard the voice of Jesus tell her, "All shall be well, and all shall be well, and all manner of things shall be well." And again, centuries later, Teresa of Ávila wrote and kept on a bookmark (love her for this), the concise wisdom of her awakening and the challenge to meet it: "Let nothing disturb you. Let nothing frighten you. All things are passing away. God never changes. Patience obtains all things. Whoever has God lacks nothing. God alone suffices."

When the existential angst creeps in, it's easy to wonder if hope is stupid. Why imagine a different kind of world? Why bother with bravery or kindness, if it's all still going to fall to shit? Why not just put your head down and try not to get in anyone's way? So many people do that. It's easier not to care or not to get too involved.

Hoping for the rise of a new day will cause you pain and suffering, I absolutely guarantee it. You will be disappointed. Your patience will wear thin. It can be excruciating to wait when your agency as an individual is minuscule. But damn if it isn't the way of spiritual truth—the long and agonizing road to something bursting forth like flowers in the spring. It is a universal truth that all will be well. It is dependable to believe that God never changes. It is radical in scope to carry such bravery in your heart, and kindness for those who have been kicked aside along the way.

TIME TO WAKE UP

Hope

In most of the recorded meetings with angels in the Hebrew Bible and Christian Scripture, the angels always start the conversation with, "Fear not." What would be possible for you if you weren't afraid? To start, try on courage for a minute, or for a day. Allow yourself to have hope that the darkest night is followed by a new day. It may take time. It may take patience. The systems of this world do gravitate toward greed and power, that's true. But what if your awakened, courageous, and vulnerable heart is one that is turning the key toward an open door to what's next? There's always a what's next. That's the promise and the gift. Your curiosity will give you eyes to see the transformations that are taking place and the courage to participate in making a difference where you can.

3

GET GOING

Great Quests Come from Great Questions

> *"I wish it need not have happened in my time,"*
> *said Frodo.*
>
> *"So do I," said Gandalf, "and so do all who live*
> *to see such times. But that is not for them to*
> *decide. All we have to decide is what to do*
> *with the time that is given us."*
>
> —J. R. R. Tolkien

ON THE SPIRITUAL JOURNEY we can find ourselves mired in the language of comparing our journey with those of others. There will always be a temptation to rank our spiritual experiences against others and try to come off sounding like a spiritually evolved person, a mystic, an intentional rebel-saint. There's a story that spiritual writer and clinical psychologist James Finley tells about the time he told his spiritual guide, renowned monk

Thomas Merton, about how he thought he had reached the spiritual stage of at least the "fourth mansion"—a level of enlightenment in a framework the mystic Teresa of Ávila outlined in her book *The Interior Castle*. Merton, listening to his mentee, looked at him, not skipping a beat, and said, "Go wash dishes."

You may feel special and chosen, sent to preach an important message of repentance to the blowhards of Nineveh. Or a spiritual counselor you trust might remind you that those who are sent on the hero's journey spend a great deal of time chopping wood, carrying water, or doing dishes. To be awakened by a quest will inevitably be humbling even if it's sometimes spectacular.

In Scripture, nearly every time God calls upon someone to get up and go, it's met with either disbelief or fear, or some combination thereof. And likely some mess. The one who is chosen will be and should be humbly afraid, afraid of what they might be asked to do or where they might be asked to go. And those who feel they are high on the mystical rungs will likely find the journey begins at the rungs of ordinary life and service and washing the dishes.

Once our pride is taken down a rung, we discover that hand in hand with this chosen-ness comes the inevitable question that is even more humbling. Our worthiness. *Who me? You really don't mean me, God, do you?* Maybe the surprise is that you won't have to prove yourself good enough to be tapped for this kind of side quest. More likely is your being tapped by God when you're feeling at your lowest rungs. Hebrew and Christian Scriptures show a God routinely making odd choices from among the most unusual suspects. The "worthy" and self-righteous and self-promoting are bypassed. But what *will* be required is your receptivity to whatever crazy adventure God has in mind, fearful or not. *Yes, God. Here I am. Sucky as I might be. Send me if you think you know what you are doing.*

To say I had no idea I was being called into ministry when I was being called into ministry is an understatement. Instead, it felt like being sent on an unlikely quest. My experience started with a "God, you've got to be kidding" moment that somehow found an unlikely trust in God's goodness building up over my formative years.

I was extraordinarily fortunate to grow up in a rural West Virginia church that welcomed my curiosity. In my small town, that kind of openness was an oddity. Not only was I allowed to ask questions, it was encouraged. I liked church and developed an appreciation for the handful of adults there who didn't talk down to me. The stories told from the pulpit kept capturing my attention even when I tried to send my mind elsewhere. There were so many dang underdogs being sent on wild and impossible journeys. Hearing those tales fed my soul like nothing else did. The young adventurer in me couldn't help but be drawn in.

But as I was nearing the end of high school and starting to think about college choices, I was paying more attention than most teens to what was really going on in religious communities around me, and I felt a hearty *No, thank you* to considering leading a church. To face the scrutiny of being a small-town pastor in a tiny fishbowl? I relish my privacy. Working on weekends? Nu-uh. I liked going out. Not getting paid much, but getting bitched at constantly? Hell no. Wouldn't be worth it. I saw the cost.

My logical plan was to studiously prepare for law school. The justice part made sense. I was already becoming outspoken and had a penchant for argument and asking big questions. I positioned myself for exactly that, except that in college I fared better with my theological logic than I did in political science. During my first poli-sci exam, I started writing on the first question, realized I had no idea what I was doing, started to sweat profusely, and got up and left the room, walking straight to the office where I would fill out the paperwork to drop the class. Not to be deterred, I thought I could pursue law from some other angle, so I applied to be a national youth delegate for our denomination. That year the assembly was in Philadelphia. It would be good for my resume, right? I could start over.

Judgey me, I arrived and started looking around, getting almost that same sweaty feeling as from my poli-sci exam. All I could see were the stupid goody-two-shoes young people who were there to do the same job I was. Unlike me, they came mostly from bigger cities—and vastly different experiences of church life. They knew the camp songs, they wanted to pray, and they kumbayahed in ways that I thought couldn't possibly be sincere.

It's probably helpful to know that drawn to the church as I was, I was a full-fledged party-girl—well on my way to trying to prove that the stereotypical Young Life persona was not for me. You don't need to know the lurid details for me to paint a picture for you. I was living through a different time, when consent was mushy at best, and the beer was always free flowing to loosen any inhibitions that might have meant better judgment. In those days, for every guy who was celebrated for sowing a few wild oats, there was a girl dabbling in the same environment, but being called slutty for the very same experimental curiosity. My college was famously proud of its reputation as a party school, and my strong desire to fit in found me a lively participant in all that the environment had to offer, with frequent bouts of shame to accompany my exploits.

Almost every powerful awakening begins with questioning the status quo. Something shifts before, well, it really shifts. By the time I set foot in the Philadelphia assembly, I was starting to not like myself very much. I was pledging a sorority, drinking most nights, and having regrettable hook-ups, all of which were making me realize that the hole I was trying to fill in my soul was just getting bigger.

I wasn't finding love and friendship the way I hoped when I first dreamed of leaving the constraints of my small-town home. I was growing increasingly more miserable. Finding myself depressed at a political assembly of Presbyterians caucusing with the overlay of a religious conference, I was nauseated by the seemingly perfect religious types—as much as I was with myself.

The identity-building project of young adulthood—that you think is so unique to you as you are going through it—can be so maddingly stereotypical. As a young adult, my common lot was to see the world in such dualistic ways and with polarized choices. You are either terribly boring and religious *or* you are the life of the party. You can't be both, and you can't be neither. Now I am grateful to see high school and college students multiplying their options beyond the old dualisms, still in formative young adult years and seeking identity clarification, but more of a spectrum of engagement—not a "this but not that" mentality. Just, *Who am I? And how will I seek to engage my world? I have to know, and know clearly.*

But strangely, this messy religious foray into my discomfort lead up to my aha moment with the Divine. One morning of that assembly, I woke up at the ass crack of dawn to go to the Peace Breakfast keynoted by William Sloane Coffin, a pastor and peacemaker someone told me to go and hear speak. I never made it to that breakfast. I was unpleasantly interrupted by a full-blown existential crisis. Up until that point I had never, ever been so mad at God in my life. As I walked there, I detoured into the women's bathroom at the conference center, and began a shouting match with God. I think it was mostly an internal conversation, but it felt very, very loud. Looking back now, I'm not 100 percent sure. There were so many swear words on both sides. And an insistence from me that I was in the wrong place, and that I was taking the next fucking train home from Philadelphia (even though as a rural kid with no city experience I couldn't have begun to know how to do that). I cried. No, I sobbed. It was ugly. And it was a very real experience of knowing God's presence with me in an absolute kind of way. I felt singled out. Chosen—but not like halos and angels singing. This was chosen in the worst possible way. I could hear God plain as can be, saying, "I want you here. And I will ask even more of you." *Shit.*

It wasn't the holy curiosity of many spiritual experiences that turns your attention toward awe and faithfulness and the radical beauty of this world. It was the absolute terror of God saying, "I choose you." Damn right, I was afraid!

Fear not? Yeah, right. That's biblical bullshit that can only be expressed *long* after the power of the encounter has passed, when there's nothing left but to trust in what was felt in that moment. I didn't know how my life would unfold—or unravel—from there, but looking back, I knew there was a quest ahead, because I walked into so many questions. *What do I have to do next? What would I need to give up?* It made me face the pain of my own life in ways I previously couldn't. I had to come to terms with the best and worst of myself, the best and worst of my desires.

By the end of that early-morning bathroom conversation, despite myself and my resistance, there was an overwhelming sense of relief that I could quit running—mostly because I suddenly knew I was never going to outrun or be able to hide from who God is.

There's a psalm about knowing and being known: Psalm 139, the one that comforts some people that begins, "O LORD, you have searched me and know me." Well, it goes on to ask the bathroom question: "Where can I go from your spirit? Where can I flee from your presence?" Some people read into it that it's about God's protection, but I read it and I hear that it's about being hunted down and cornered right where God wanted me to be.

I get it. I get why the prophets just don't want to go. I get why Jonah not only got swallowed by the whale but was then spit up again on shore. That's what it feels like to be chosen. You can run down a long list of those who were selected for the holy quest who struggled with their callings. And you can also look into the past of any saint and see the mess, the resistance, the hell-nos.

Fun fact. Paul, whose opinionated letters are published in the Bible of all places, got his start torturing and executing Christians before his awakening. And John Newton, who wrote the words of the beloved hymn "Amazing Grace," was first a slave trader before his big turnaround. A wretch like me? Now you know.

But the change doesn't always take place right after a brush with blindness or death. You get an invitation. A shake-up—but you still have a choice. I didn't immediately stop partying and learn how to be the good-girl Christian I thought came with the territory of being chosen. That's not how human lives work.

Transformation isn't one-time, it's something that goes on for the full length of the game. It's not something set up for quick resolution. My chasing after happiness and wholeness continued along its rocky path, and it took a lot of personal healing to reconcile the behaviors that were numbing and reckless from the desire every human being has for being loved and accepted exactly as they are. (And believe me, there's a whole lifetime worth of work to be done on that issue!)

What I did learn, though, and continued to learn was that you get a moment of awakening and you'll be asked to grow and change. I've always been annoyed by the people who say, "God may love you exactly as you are, but God loves you too much to let you stay that way." But a manifestation of the hero's journey is being sent on the quest. The beginning of the trip is only that: the beginning. It's a big event. And then you do dishes. What you learn and do and who you meet along the way are why you get tapped to be sent in the first place. You may not even know yourself well enough to imagine what kind of hero you will become.

Pretty common, after you return to doing dishes, is just figuring out what only a minute ago happened to you, what *this* is. You begin gathering information. There is a gamer quality to this. You start asking other characters you meet along the way how the story is supposed to go. Maybe you take classes, change careers, start a project, seek wisdom. I started taking more of the religion classes I liked and was good at. I looked at pursuing a theological education. I interned in a church. I applied to seminary. And because you are never done awakening, there I experienced almost an exact repeat of what had happened at the assembly. I found myself surrounded by even more happy-clappy Christians. God, this was the worst. And yet there I was also *stunned* to find myself joyfully immersed in long-dead languages and riveted even by the minutia of the most argumentative theological conversations.

Eventually I found my people, even though I felt like a misfit for quite some time. Oh, those shiny happy Christians are still there to be my ongoing nemesis in the land of institutional religion, but I consider myself to be in the good company of Jesus whenever I whisper the word "hypocrite" under my breath. To be a leader on this chosen journey is to find yourself among both the suck-ups and the fuck-ups in just about every location.

Maybe that's a good thing: to be both skeptical of the religious part and truly engaged by the human-longing-for-God part. I often wonder what happens to those ministers and chaplains and do-gooders who have not had their come-to-Jesus moment flooded by tears in a bathroom stall in the Philadelphia convention center. How can you trust a God that has no capacity to scare the absolute shit out of you? It's not exactly a career path you take for the money—unless you are truly willing to rip off widows and wipe out the savings accounts of the poor whom you find ways to bamboozle. To know and trust a God you can hurl your anger and grief and pain at is to know a different kind of God than the God of corny songs at the lock-in.

So, fast-forwarding through my first decade of ministry: no sainthood here. I never quite lost the hunger of wanting to be important, known, influential, and dare I say it, *loved* by a huge flock of people. I was on the same track as other professional clergy—do well—and then apply for bigger and "better" churches. Climb the ladder of ecclesial success to merit the love of God and everyone else too.

But when God chooses you, it isn't like being smiled on as you climb ecclesial rungs. It's usually more— the opposite. You have to pay attention to the minor consolations, the small victories, the serendipitous moments when God's presence seems close, again. Because the path of descent is real. That ladder you find doesn't really go up. Following the journey God sets out for you will have major twists and a lot of nasty requirements. It's messy and it sucks.

And it isn't just that I haven't even made the lowest salary I would have made as a lawyer in the jobs I've taken. It's that I have routinely been sent into situations that seemed hopeless, but now with the expectation that I would retell those same stories of transformation that captured my attention from a very young age, such that others would be transformed by hearing them. Could I tell stories of God's deliverance knowing that so many people are still being held in chains? Could I preach resurrection—and mean it? And believe it? And expect it to happen among regular people? Why did I keep getting sent into captivity, conflict, death, and mountains of bureaucratic bullshit?

Because I am, and we are, on the precipice of a much larger, much more significant awakening than just a little public bathroom moment with the Divine would have me imagine when transformation is occurring, that God does what God does, and gathers up all the misfits around the margins to bring down what's been rotting away in the center. You're not called just for you. You're called into spiritual action for more-than-you.

I'm beginning to think that about every decade or so, I come due for a God-booster of my Philadelphia revelation. The fear of being sent on a quest by God wears off a bit. I'd get complacent, maybe a little bit cozy even with the status quo of my own life. Sure, being a pastor has its ups and downs. It's the people mostly. I was no longer trying to escape the quest, though, but I was trying to climb up to a vantage point where it wouldn't be so damn hard anymore. One ticket to easy-town, please. It's like the song from *Book of Mormon* where the young missionary sings his prayer to God to be sent to his most favorite place in the world: Orlando. The longing for it to be easier, or maybe even over, starts to make sense. It's how you get ministers going through the motions, who are boring to listen to, who stay in it for the pension, and who are trying so very hard not to rock the boat. You know it, too. They may not be awful, but they certainly aren't engaged either. They are among the multiple reasons why the church can't possibly be the only place where spiritual awakenings happen!

So again, I started looking for wisdom and spoke with a pastor in my area whom many considered a pariah—a man who had left his formal ordination untouched for years in order to hold sweat lodge retreats in the woods. *Maybe this Yoda figure would have some words of insight,* I thought. I sat on his dilapidated couch in a musty old building seeking answers. Perhaps by now I should expect that being tapped on the shoulder by God will smell like must, or urine, or sweat, or straight-up anxiety. Though no certainty was forthcoming, I did get a profound question to help me on my quest. I was bitching about religion and all its trappings, and whining about wanting to be more spiritually awesome, and he said to me, "You've been called to this, right?" I said, "Yes." Then he asked me, "What did you say 'yes' to?"

Great quests ultimately start with great questions. *What did you say yes to?*

That's a lifelong kind of exploration. What *did* you say yes to?

I have, shall we say, *experience* with the word "no." Trying to climb the ladder of success in the church? You'll commonly hear the word "no." There are the polite nos that come in letters and emails. There are the nos that hurt because you really thought you wanted some job or some accolade. And there are the hell-nos that remind you that God may just know you better than you know yourself. You catch a glimpse of what you thought you wanted to do, how you wanted people to look at you as someone with power and authority, and you cringe and remember, *That's not what I said yes to.*

God's yes is enigmatic. Those on the quest notice the clues and crumbs that are being left for you to notice. The old mystics call these crumble stuffs "consolations." You know you are being consoled by God along the way when you get that message from the universe at just the right time. You know, because it answers the deep questions of your heart. These serendipitous moments were what a former parishioner called "divinely coordinated coincidences." What captures your attention may only have meaning to you—but you hear the lyrics of a song as an affirmation of your direction, or you end up at just the right place in just the right time such that it feels like the Divine has orchestrated that moment just for you. Then you know you aren't merely wandering on your own. You've been sent!

What is most important about the quest's power to awaken you is knowing deep down that your experience matters. It matters that God chose *you*. Particularly you. The you that has the you-ness that you like, and the you that has the you-ness that you hate. As Teresa of Ávila writes in *The Interior Castle*, when we experience God's presence in a significant, life-changing moment, it will be accompanied by a copious amount of tears. She nailed that one. When I have felt closest to God, my body reacted as much as my mind or spirit. Snotty, ugly tears. Don't-look-at-me tears. And I suspect that, depending on the person, whatever feelings there are in that moment, they will be amplified. That's the overpowering nature of being sent.

And think about how radical that truly is. To understand that individuals are sent on these spiritual journeys to learn, to change, and to grow is to not only imagine but to believe that God is in real relationship with human beings. *That's* what happens along the way.

But wait! My storyline is only one example of how the quest might get played out—gamer style. *Your* character is your own, with different strengths, armor, style, and tactics for the journey. The exceptional news is that the Holy One knows exactly what type of spiritual journey you need to undertake. You may be led through anger instead of tears or joy instead of frustration. You may be following what would seem to me like imperceptible crumbs when mine needed to practically be slices of bread to get my eyes to open. The path, as the Buddhists say, is made by walking, and I can't do your walking for you, and you couldn't have done my walking for me. You may feel like you are being sent around the globe or only down the street. What matters for the events of your life to become a quest isn't how far you are willing to go, but how willing you are to ask the questions that open you up to the journey of transformation. Those highs and lows of your own life will change you, precisely because they are the turning points of your journey.

The quest begins with the question "Who, me?" or "Why me?" Or, maybe, "Wait, what?" A change in the landscape requires something else. You are low in the valley and want to climb out of it. You are high on the mountaintop but feel all alone. A feeling comes from somewhere that is both you and not you, telling you it's time to move on. For me, it felt like I had to quit running away and start on the path toward. I went from thinking, *I can escape this*, to *I can experience this*. Is this the work of God or just my own discomfort with the status quo? I guess there's no perfect way of being sure, yet dodging the questions didn't feel like a viable option. So on the quest, I went.

The awakening asks for a response: the journey itself. The odyssey. The pilgrimage. The outward actions and the introspection. Maybe the quester has the sense of,

"Go where I tell you. Do as I ask you." Maybe it sounds more like, *Shift in this way*. Or, *Pay attention to that person, who needs your help right now*. My personal quest was a reorientation. I had to quit climbing some rung of an imagined success ladder and surrender to being led on a journey that I would neither control nor completely understand. Rather than follow my own drive alone, I felt like I had both divine and human interventions that accompanied me on my journey.

And when you awaken, get shaken up, say yes, and begin the quest? You will be drawn deeper into trusting the crumbs, coincidences, and companions that you will find along this journey, even if you aren't completely sure where it's headed. There's no more running. Nothing left to prove. The secret sauce is being surrendered by being awake and alive to all that is happening in your very own life.

For me, that is a holy gift. Worth all my gratitude. All in. And there's likely more mess to come, because this is a scandal, a big one at that. All in, as the mystical side of the apostle Paul teaches, means nothing can separate you from the love of God: nothing. The life you have is the life you are meant to have. You can't live another. But we all try to do that anyway, right? That's why the yes, the quest, the surrender is ongoing.

Surrender is a practice. It never quits being hard. Most religions don't teach it, because very few religious practitioners are able to imagine that it will *work*. After nearly thirty years of learning how to see God's light shed on particular moments—after falling and licking my wounds and getting back up again—I would be led to the experience that would give me what I would call "full access" to such unitive consciousness, to experience what I had always longed for, what I felt like I was saying yes to, and what I believe is the desire in God reaching out to the desire for God already in me. That would only be present for me when I was able to utterly let go of everything about the identity I had built and worked so hard to form and know. That meant going beyond knowledge of myself and being drenched in the knowledge of God. But that was still to come.

In the journey of spiritual awakening, inevitably there will be questions as you follow, and some will involve being sent ... somewhere—to do ... something. Here are a few questions and thoughts to start you pondering about your own journey.

TIME TO WAKE UP

Who Am I?

God knows you as you, so what is it about you that makes you the right person for this particular quest?

Are you good with words? Do you make friends easily? Do you have a skill, a virtue, or a character trait that is being used for the good of others?

What is it about you that might seem problematic, but oddly makes you sympathetic to the task at hand? Are you fantastic at cutting through organizational BS? Are you able to see the pain in the heart of a bully because you once were one?

Why Am I Here?

We as human beings are bound by time and space. You are here, now. Why here, why now?

What Did I Say Yes To?

Whether it is saying "yes" to letting your kids know they are loved or learning as much microbiology as you can in hopes of curing cancer—the path that lights up for you is your quest if it is leading you into a deeper relationship with yourself, with the Divine, or for the greater benefit of others. Does your yes feel like it has a purpose?

There's no one right path to suit everyone, and there may not even be a singular path for you. You might be a parent who loves microbiology and find that both are incredibly important to your spiritual transformation. What moves your heart to say, "Yes"? Have you ever named it? Doubted it? Followed it? Surrendered to that yes?

What Difference Does My Life Make?

Ponder a time you committed to making a difference, small or large, to produce outcomes that change something, anything, for the better. Did you find you've done that in similar, multiple ways? Did you notice a pattern? Maybe in that pattern you may have found your life's purpose. I believe the Holy One loves co-creating with us in the unfolding of life for the good.

Now consider a time you've made a decision to say no to what your inner voice seemed to be telling you and instead climb the rungs of ladders that others built in the name of success? Did you see the difference your choice made? Did it have harmful consequences for others?

Remember, we get multiple chances to hear how life is beckoning us on the spiritual journey, but at times we feel like taking a pass. Maybe we need rest to go at it another day, or maybe we are actively resisting what the universe is trying to tell us. But when we choose those things that we know will hurt or injure others, experiencing judgment through a consequence of some kind is likely to be the jab you need to pay attention. When the going gets tough, and it's messy to get back on track, try not to dismiss those harder aspects of your quest. The difference you might make is by deciding not to make that hurtful comment or not to act out toward others because you have found yourself in a low place.

4

PICK A LANE
Choosing My Religion

Believing takes practice.

—Madeleine L'Engle

THE UNIVERSE IS VAST and incomprehensible in its completeness. We barely get enough time on this planet to get a good glimpse of who we are, let alone gain understanding or even appreciation for the whole concept of life in its diversity and abundance. To even start comprehending our world and our place in it, we need a variety of tools. Religion is, at its best, one such tool.

You aren't the first person ever to go out in search of meaning. More than likely, a few people ahead of you will have had some insights or guidance to help you make spiritual sense of your own life. As through centuries and sometimes millennia, religions have learned and changed and grown in their own comprehension, they carry the insights through history that have shaped their recognition of patterns, practices, and the questions that are shaped by and speak to the human experience.

Religion has been one of the longest-lived ways to address the role of persons in the expanding knowledge of the universe. Through religion and its intersection with story, poetry, prayer, ritual, art, music, and exploration, we learn about our humanity. We practice our humanity through morality that teaches us to be kind, compassionate, and fair. We experience our humanity when we discover who we are in relationships with each other, ourselves, nature, and the spiritual world. We awaken to the whole the deeper we go in each of these arenas of life.

And through history, religion has intersected and engaged with an astounding number of fields: science, philosophy, psychology, anthropology, sociology, and more. Unlike other fields that have often limited their study, religion has often expanded its insights specifically because those who practice their faith want to know how to engage the world fully. It's an important lens through which to understand our place in the world because of that widened engagement.

As we together explore religion's power for guiding a spiritual awakening, it's important for you to know that I come from a religious tradition (Christianity) that informs my practice of spirituality. It's what I know best, so it will be what pops up most often and with the greatest depth of expression. There's a reason for that. I have chosen, repeatedly, to return to what Christianity has to teach me because I have allowed it to lay its claim on my life. I therefore find myself wrestling deeply with its unhinged moments on the days when I'd rather call myself anything but a Christian. But it's also important for me to identify that I don't feel so *exclusive* in my practice of religion either. I am more polyreligious, or pluralistic, in my approach. I will beg, borrow, or steal from any religion's truths to help me understand my spirituality better. Barbara Brown Taylor identifies this approach in her book *Holy Envy*, in which she takes her collegiate Intro to Religion students on field trips to a variety of religious services and rituals and finds herself envious of the aspects of faith she finds more compelling from traditions other than her own. I love to learn about all the religions, all the practices, all the idiosyncrasies of living a faithful life, and I don't feel guilty at all about my lack of religious monogamy. However, drawing from less familiar traditions where my knowledge is shallow can sometimes leave me feeling like an interloper because I only scratch the surface of understanding what it means to be Buddhist or Jewish or Hindu.

Intentionality is important if religion's going to be a guide for a person's spiritual life. That sounds like a no-brainer, but what that means for me is that blind faith won't be of much value on the spiritual journey. Picking a religious lane can make it possible to go deeper, because rather than your faith being something handed over to you, you permit it to become the worldview that makes its claim on you. You decide you are going to *believe* in it. Many religions have a specific ritual designed for exactly this—when you accept the mantle of your tradition as a guidepost for how you will live your life. In contrast, an unconsidered or unexamined religious outlook will just have you doubling down on what you were taught by whoever benefits most from you staying in line with what that particular religious tradition teaches. In time, you will be given the opportunity (as with spiritual awakening) to choose or release what has been handed to you by way of the tradition that leaves its mark on you. Maybe you'll do some of both. That's when it gets personal.

As I consider the impact that choosing Christianity has had on me, my vows of ordination to the ministry stand out as a prime example of how I intentionally committed my life to standing in a particular tradition. Even among Christians, the process for becoming a religious leader can differ, but one of the questions I was asked when I made that commitment was, "Do you accept the Scriptures of the Old and New Testaments to be, by the Holy Spirit, the unique and authoritative witness to Jesus Christ in the Church universal, and God's Word to you?" *God's Word—to you*. Like many other traditions, mine happens to be based on a book. Not movies. Not commentaries on books. Not podcasts on spiritual self-help related to that book. This book has a history, and though affirming that history is part of the role of a religious leader, it isn't all that's required. I deeply appreciate that, in my tradition, I am not asked to affirm Scripture's inerrancy or claim that "God said it in the King's English, so I believe it. That's the final word." I was asked, in my own tradition's way, to be reflective about how I approach my tradition's sacred text. It's one of my favorite things about that question. It allows my tradition space to breathe.

That breathing room is everything for me. Or else, as one of my congregants used to enjoy saying, I would merely become a shit merchant for the cause. There are not only religious people but religious teachers out there who only see the prejudices that have been handed down to them through certain interpretations of what they have read or been taught. For them, their book or their way becomes a marketing tool, a sales pitch that only says what they want it to say. Those clergy always, *always*, have something they are trying to sell, and not only are those platitudes and gimmicks not worth buying, they also stink.

Despite all those times when religion becomes stagnant or gimmicky, I still believe there are opportunities for awakening to be found along a religious path. When you actively and consciously choose to follow a well-worn tradition, it opens up the way for seeing differently from when you are just following the ways of your personal ancestors and teachers with no application of critical thought. And, friends, I am less concerned with *which* path you choose than *that* you choose one—for *you*. And if choosing a land and going deeply down one path and making it your own puts you in a panic around choice, rest assured that it also oddly creates more appreciation for the wisdom and truth in other paths than if you skim along the surface with religion merely being a confirmation of the prejudices and cultural adaptations you already find comforting.

Religion should disturb you. Often. If it doesn't wreck your day or rock your world every now and then, there's little power to be found in it. Perhaps you will find yourself on the path that hasn't been plowed enough. Every religion has its own brand of superficial fundamentalism that is packed down so hard that no seed will take root in it. Or maybe you will find that you haven't let it get into your bones deep enough to begin to grow in you. If this is the case, rather than giving up, it may be the time to ask questions and learn more. Stay or leave it, but choose the direction you go in—for you.

So, given that most people who claim to be religious say they belong to the sect of their upbringing, is religion something we *can* choose? I still belong to the branch of Christianity that claimed me through the practice of infant baptism. I didn't choose to be baptized. My parents chose that for me. They took me to the church they belonged to. The pastor put water on my head and blessed me in the name of the Triune God—Father, Son, and Holy Spirit. Was that moment what made me who I am in any spiritual sense? The answer is probably yes and no. Yes, the church my parents took me to is the church that formed me. But no, there were many divergent choices along the way that made me both indebted to and separate from the spiritual life of my childhood.

Some say religion, therefore, is simply a matter of fate. I was destined to be a Christian, if you will. My own tradition would find that both truthful and humorous! In some regards, my choices were, in fact, limited. And that's okay too. I don't need every single option available to me to begin to form my identity—religious or otherwise. If I were born to Indian parents in Calcutta instead of taking my first breath in rural Maryland, I probably would not find myself as a member of one of America's rapidly declining Protestant religious communities. But within that framework, I have options.

Sometimes religious adherence is generational, even to the point of being assumed that it's inherited from parents. "My mother was Buddhist so now that means I'm Buddhist too." Or it could be a decision driven by differences in a marriage but chosen so that both partners agree to the compromise. "We chose to be Presbyterian because one of us was Baptist and the other one was Catholic, so it seemed a good middle ground." It could be a decision to reject the tradition of your formative years as no longer relevant. "My parents were conservative, evangelical Christians, and I didn't like that structure, so now I'm a humanist Unitarian."

Of course, given the current statistical rise of the "nones," many people want to say that they choose spirituality instead of a religious tradition or make the choice to be of no religion whatsoever. However, some impulses associated with religion just might be innate to life—especially larger-brained mammalian life. Take, for instance, how the great apes and elephants have their own ways to honor their dead. And it's becoming more widely accepted to believe that our beloved cats and dogs really do appreciate us—and maybe even love us. These impulses are true to what it means to be alive. We create. We express. We show concern. We make connections with others "like us." We bond over the cycle of birth, life, and death in creaturely ways. So, really, just how "none" can we be? I'm not sure. Most of us are probably more "some" when it comes to religion. Let me make the case for that in considering what religion can do to inspire and awaken human life. Although we may think we are choosing to be religious (or not), perhaps it also is true that the religious impulse chooses to come alive in us.

Given that my family, my culture, and my history play a role in my being religious, this choice I have is less about selecting from the biggest possible menu of options than it is about choosing the teachings of my faith and allowing them to guide and shape who I am becoming. When I say that I am choosing my religion, it means that I am continually and consciously recommitting myself to its patterns, practices, and way of life. Faith therefore becomes important to how I choose to live.

And right now you might be thinking, *Religion sucks. I want to run as far away from it as possible.* But here you are reading a book that might hold some clue about what it could mean for you. I get it. I won't try to make the case for religion being wonderful in all or even most of its expressions. Religious zealotry has caused wars and justified genocide. Religion's lust for power enabled the possibility for caste-based hierarchical thinking. This devaluation of human life led to the possibility for human enslavement in ancient times and escalated through more modern times as the superiority of Christian colonial masters kept it going and tied it to the amount of a body's melanin. And, yes, religious "purity" tends to condemn any deviation from the norm, and the ones hurt most by this alienating and scapegoating in our own time are the LGBTQ+ community.

And these are just a few of religion's more problematic associations. I fully understand what makes people think it's all a load of shit. More on the benefits of losing your religion in the next chapter, so if you identify as someone who has been pummeled by religion, hang on for a few more pages. I'll show where religion might offer some possibilities for sparking an awakening, and for seeing how the enduring truths that persist beyond religious scandal might light up your path and lead you toward spiritual transformation.

Religion Is Messy

Religion can teach its followers to grow and act in positive ways, toward a collective purpose and a greater sense of unity. There are ways to see with fresh eyes that religious patterns, practices, and insights do point to the greater truth that so many of us are seeking. And there are ways even now that religious principles and practices are bringing about individual and cultural awakenings. Sometimes you have to see the mess of religion first to then see more clearly where the mess isn't.

Learning a religion may be like learning a language: your earliest exposure is often what you have learned best (for better or worse). Yes, you may want to run, but consider taking your first dance with the religious partner that brought you to this place of exploration. You can always choose to learn more about a different religion or religions later. But to dismiss a tradition out of hand is its own mess and doesn't allow you to interact with it in this adulting way, this way of choice. For a religious tradition to matter to you, it's important to pick a path and go deeply. And no matter what your early teachings in the tradition have been, there is no requirement that you always agree with the religion you have chosen. Sometimes disagreement is the struggle to make it better. The most profound religious leaders have done the same, including leaders like Martin Luther King Jr. and Nelson Mandela, who challenged the racism of cultural Christianity; or a leader like Ghandi, who challenged the caste system as an opposition to the truth about human worth; or the countless women and members of the LGBTQ+ community who demanded recognition and ordination when they were not given access to the authority of their traditions. Jesus didn't set out to make *Christian* followers. He was deeply tied to his own formative Jewish beliefs. And you don't need to either bend yourself or change anyone else's religion to your own to understand and be gracious toward other practitioners. In fact, it's far better that you don't. My rabbi friend prays for me on my Christian journey, and I pray for him to continue to inspire his Jewish community. No conversion necessary.

To have a religion wake you up and come alive for you, don't merely assent to what someone tells you is true about it. Transformation is about choosing and making up your own mind. That kind of choosing and discernment comes from learning the religion's history. Practice its rituals. Ask that tradition questions. What does your religion teach about the nature of the Divine? What does it mean to be human and to be moral according to your religion's practices of living?

Shuck open shell after shell in your tradition until you find its pearl of great price. Don't settle for just the cheap trinkets. Paying attention to the patterns, practices, and insights will help you awaken to the beauty others before you have seen and now pass on to you. When you choose your religion, you join a stream of others who have so much to offer to the generations coming after you. A living tradition is always far more understanding, helpful, and wise than a dead one.

Religious Patterns

On the surface, all clerical shit merchants are the same. They follow the pattern of the "false prophets," to use a biblical term. They are the *users* of religion. They will tell you that religion, *their* religion, is the one thing that is going to make your life better. However, it's usually a façade to get you to make their lives better. The prosperity preachers, who are my favorites to hate on, do their little song and dance to have you think that if you dedicate your life (meaning your money) to God (meaning to them), you will have a full on *#blessed* experience for all your living days—and when you die, heaven will be your perfect reward. And if heaven isn't good enough, imagining your enemies rotting in hell can be a pretty powerful motivator as well. But probe deeper, and religion isn't *only that*—and even hardly that at all. Religion is and always will be about negotiating the suck of life, but you only find out how when you go deeper. That's where you discover the merchants selling the happy-clappy bullshit as seen on TV are selling some version they made up.

The true patterns that show up time and again in the full expression of religious storytelling are about human survival—sometimes under the very worst conditions life has to dish out. If your religion falls flat when times get tough—ditch it. Quickly. Or at least look again at what it's trying to teach you. The sanitized Sunday school lesson you heard when you were eight is likely not enough for living through the crushing greed of late-stage capitalism or the grasping zealotry of those who fight to preserve their favorite privileges and save their upper-tier place in social hierarchies. Such economic hardships and political corruption can be found in every age. Pandemics and catastrophic natural events—also in every age. Moronic leaders and the destructive wars that make such leaders feel potent appear throughout history. Large numbers of oppressed and marginalized people, you guessed it: every age has them. We think we are living through the worst time—ever. Well, history will be quite happy to say to you, "Hold my beer."

Your mundane pattern of existence? The smartass teacher in the biblical book of Ecclesiastes tells us that it's all vanity. You have no choice in the matter. You are born, you live, you work, you suffer, you die—and most, if not all, of it will suck. But religions add a twist or two to that equation. It is *also true* that you have been gifted by the Creator with at least some possibilities for living out your life well. It is *also true* that death does not get the final word. All religions have something to say about the kind of renewal that is greater than and surpasses death. It can be rebirth, resurrection, reincarnation—or another set of re-somethings. You get to die, even in this life, and go toward something more beyond it, literally and figuratively.

So, this enduring pattern of birth, life, death, and renewal becomes charged with meaning and assigned value through religious narratives that attempt to address the pain we associate with struggle, loneliness, loss, and fear. While our beginnings and endings are a given, we want to know that what happens in between has purpose. Religion has told and retold the stories meant to answer the big questions: *How can I possibly believe God is good when my own life feels like a three-ring shit show? How can I love my neighbor when I can't even love myself? If everything is out of my control, what good is it to even try to be part of what Judaism names the* tikkun olam, *the repair of the world?* Religious patterns, dare I say the deepest religious truths, are meant to address the most frustrating and persistently unanswerable existential questions. Thank God. Because these are the stories that will speak to the heart and change it—for the better.

So, for the record, I have no PhD in comparative religion to lend me clout in proving this point. I cannot exhaustively tell you that all religious narratives will be equally helpful. My guess is they're not. Some answers might make sense in the present moment and then raise more questions a week from now. But I trust that the long-standing religions that have stood the test of time have the potential for being good companions for your spiritual walk, especially at their depths, and especially when they can be separated from those that use their faith and traditions as a tool for manipulation.

It helps to let go of a naivete that assumes that just because someone quotes the Bible or says they believe in God, they are being sincere. I know that some groups that claim to be God-centered and truth-based seem very far from either. Religions fall out of practice and die when the stories they tell no longer connect people to the greater truth the stories are yearning to describe. Religion is strange like that. You can historically study dead ones, but it would be a lesson in futility to try to resuscitate them. A religion that is alive will connect living, breathing people to the pattern of life itself in such a way as to transcend the despair that so much about living still sucks. In this sense, religion is to know more about the human condition and its connection to the spirit and in the unitive force that holds it all together.

What is certainly not unique to me in pointing this out, but should be said here, is that good religion can be very, very good for the soul, and bad religion is—no joke—the absolute worst. Good religion will be defined by its power to captivate and speak directly to the heart of humankind. It will move you. It will humble you. It will spur you into action. If you find in your tradition the stories that help you love your neighbor more, such that Mr. Rogers would approve, yeah, dig deeper into that. Religious texts in their fullness ought to be grounded in something far bigger and more encompassing than what suits my personal desires. Good religion has to be good for more than just you, which means that religions worth practicing do justice, love kindness, and offer compassion. They unite more than they divide. They teach their adherents to live in the mess of life, seeking to discern good from evil, and counsel in making it right when inevitably we fuck things up. They acknowledge patterns that bend the trajectory of life toward transformation. They are hopeful in the midst of despair, angry in the midst of injustice, grateful for times of peace, and overjoyed when love shows up, even in the smallest of ways. They will have the power to awaken the human spirit through how they tell the story of what being human means.

When I see how the truth shows up in religious patterns that are inclusive and centered on both divine and human connection, the answers that superficial religion comes up with can be hard to take. Sure, they might be inspirational in a live-laugh-love kind of way. But the reality and truth of the patterns require study, questioning, and study again. Deliverance may come after centuries of fighting slavery, and even then, finding the safety of home can be a moving target. Salvation comes only after the innocent one suffers a humiliating trial and public execution. Enlightenment comes only by casting off all attachments, even the significant ones that seem impossible to release. These patterns are never, ever about getting exactly what we want. They are about paying attention to what changes us for the better.

And yet, the mess: these transformations are the result of pain. Most folks are more eager to place blame on their circumstances (*I don't deserve this*) or make utterly self-serving moves (*I completely deserve this*), rather than acquiesce to these patterns of truth bearing witness to life's problems.

TIME TO WAKE UP

When has religion shown up as good for you? Did it startle you or surprise you? Did it feel hard? Did it encourage you to see the world differently or to reach out to a neighbor?

What are the re-somethings you believe in? Renewal? Reincarnation? Rebirth?

When has religion been bad for you? Have you been duped by false religion? How did that feel? Were you angry? Hurt? Betrayed?

Jesus and Siddhartha Gautama would like a word here. They both were frustrated by those who wanted them to be something they couldn't be, so they created their own breathing space within the larger tradition. Seeing them as innovators can be enlightening.

Religious Practices

For a moment, let's imagine that you can separate yourself from any previously formed opinions about religion and truly be an outside observer of religious practices, with no preconceived notions whatsoever. I daresay that a rather large number of religious rituals would come off as incredibly horrifying. Take, for example, the most common Christian religious practice: Mass, the Lord's Supper, Communion. It entails the followers eating flesh and drinking blood, something that the Netflix series *Midnight Mass* with its vampiric priest denoted quite successfully for the strangeness that it truly is. And the symbol of Christianity, the cross, worn as necklaces by kids in youth groups everywhere, was the device of criminal punishment also meant to signify the full impact of Roman power and terror. One of my religious studies professors in college used to tell his classes that if Jesus were to be executed today, perhaps the Christians in the class would wear symbolic electric chairs around their necks. In Judaism, the sacred celebration of Passover denotes the time that God committed mass murder of Egyptian infants and toddlers. Sure, it was the ultimate plague that allowed the Hebrew slaves to be delivered a new land, but at a rather terrifying cost. Oh, and that savasana pose you love at the end of your yoga class? That's death practice, or in English, "corpse pose." We have always made our offerings to the gods from a sense of personal sacrifice. And we keep replaying those rituals, even when we aren't so conscious about what they actually mean.

When we practice our religion, we enact the fragility of our mortality in the presence of the immortal. We claim death and decay in our realm for the promise of life and renewal in the realm that is eternal. We are fundamentally calling upon holiness to transform us with what we do. And we do so as we sing or pray or read holy texts or interpret those texts for our own edification. We are practicing what it is like to die.

At first, it seems rather morbid. But when we see it that way, it puts life and all its mess into a much broader perspective. If a long, good life lasts a hundred years, what is it to imagine the scope of a thousand years, or ten thousand years, or a million years? When we die, will we have made a difference? Will we have pleased the gods adequately?

These are the big thoughts religion has. But then there are the littler thoughts that matter in our everyday existence. I pray to something or someone bigger than myself so that I can know, really know, that I am not God, nor will I ever be God. Prayer is the humility of the pray-er to know that there are things they cannot change—but maybe in this world they can be changed: a change enacted through prayer, through communing our desperation and hopes (and other things) to God. Prayer changes us. It takes courage to pray knowing that you aren't just asking God to do stuff. You are asking God to mold who you are.

While prayer is among the main rituals, especially in Christian tradition, there are a multitude of religious practices too numerous to mention, and religious groups divide themselves according to their practices all the time. One group claims the right way to do whatever, and then they part ways with those who are, in their view, obviously getting it wrong. I don't fault religion too much for that. To be taught a practice and experience its repetition in familiar ways forms mental pathways that enable direct access to something comforting in times of stress. Why did then-president Barack Obama publicly sing "Amazing Grace" at the funeral for Rev. Clementa Pinckney following the mass shooting at Mother Emanuel AME Church in Charleston, South Carolina? He didn't do it because he had such a talented voice that it would make others forget their pain. He did it because it was a direct line to the pain that all the mourners were collectively feeling at the time. It was a prescient moment that I don't think was premeditated. That's what religious practices can offer—almost a shortcut to the spiritual realm. And that is grace. These practices are formative and meaningful, long, long after the novelty of learning them has worn off. Humility is required to see, know, and accept that.

And yes, religious practice is boring. Repetitive. Three times a day. Weekly. Daily. And maybe it doesn't seem related to anything having to do with your regular life. But so is learning a sport. Repetitive. Early mornings. Trainings. Or how about practicing an instrument? Doing a page of math problems? Reading for knowledge?

Religious practice isn't entertainment. It isn't meant to be. Some parts, yes, should engage your spirit and be designed to wake up your mind and heart, but it isn't just about making you feel good. It's about learning how to be spiritually plugged in even when you aren't turned on. It's learning how to access the codes so that they are ready for you when you need them. You remember a story, repeat a prayer, hum a familiar song, sit and calm your mind. It takes—guess what?—*practice*.

Finding spiritual peace and rest happens in and through religious practice. And maybe like me, you don't know how to spiritually rest without knowing some rituals, traditional stories, art, and music in which to find comfort. There's something about the familiarity of things like bread and wine and water becoming more than what they seem. Maybe you light a candle or create a soft space in your favorite room. Rest in that. Sometimes, it is exactly in looking at the familiar in a new way or state of being that allows us to call upon it for fresh meaning. The best rituals and symbols can do that. They are always a changeable canvas on which we reflect who we are in the moment.

⏲ TIME TO WAKE UP

How might you "practice" death? What are the rituals you do to mark endings and new beginnings? How might they awaken you more fully to your own life?

What are your ways of praying? There are so, so many ways of conversing with the Divine. There is no one right way of doing it, so whatever method leads you to more openness and connectedness—that's the right one for you. And if what you are doing now isn't working, try something completely different. If quiet isn't working, try loud. If stillness isn't working, try movement. If going to church isn't working, spend time in nature. Or you can flip any of these as well.

Religious Insights

"Tell the truth, but tell it slant," Emily Dickinson wrote. I think the same holds true for religious insight, which often appears in riddles and parables. It's mysterious and perplexing. It's definitely slant. And for those who want certainty, the greater depths of truth will be elusive. But it's an invitation to discover the transformative and the wild. Like wild creatures that are skittish until you can stop and slowly pay attention, it is then the wild creatures, the insights, that will show themselves to you.

That's the pretty part of religious openings. Love must be revealed. It takes time. If you have time and patience, you are in luck. Religious insight will be your friend.

But if you happen to live in today's fast-paced world that rarely gives us enough time to do anything worthwhile without some interrupting notification, then something else is going to become alarmingly true for you, and it won't feel good. You may be slowed down to pay attention. The other revelation that comes through religion happens when we can't sit still, when we have screwed up badly, when the shit has hit the fan. And then, when one turns to religion for a spark of truth, a nugget of comfort, what we hear ringing loudly in our ears is a humility-making self-accusation: "You suck." We thought it was other people who sucked, but no, it turns out, we are part of the very same crowd. We are sinners, deplorables, wretches, ungrateful miserable childish assholes.

Enter sin. You know it. I know it. We can try to cover it up as mistakes or misguidance, but it's really about us in all our unawareness messing up everything. Ugh, the realization. People really, genuinely suck. And all those people you've been angrily pointing at over the years, well, it turns out that you are just as awful as they are. And your way of looking at the world does not matter. It does not discriminate between liberals and conservatives or allow one religious group to hold themselves above others as being better than. It does not matter if you've only fantasized about doing something awful, or if you've actually done the thing. To learn the truth about humanity is to recognize our collective flaws, to be keenly aware of how we hurt each other repeatedly, even when we don't want to.

That's the part of spiritual awakening that we don't often discuss. We talk about experiencing awe and feeling chosen and knowing we are loved, but rarely do we say that our awareness that God is real came to us through a kick in the ass. A few old curmudgeonly theologian types are on top of this. John Calvin made a very big deal of how totally depraved humans are. The twelve-step recovery groups know this process well. Surrender to one's powerlessness over addiction. That's a good start for the spiritual journey—hitting rock bottom. But it's true. Knowing one's lowliness sets a tone for recognizing our oneness, how we all really are in this together and equally screwed. Later we'll go deeper into this darkness as we explore the spiritual path of suffering—the dark night of the soul.

A common problem with singing the praise of whatever God or gods you've chosen to worship occurs when you become fully aware that good people may or may not be rewarded in this life, and evil jerks may or may not be punished. How can a good God, we ask, participate in such randomness?

And let me tell you, every faith has some sort of completely unsatisfying answer to this question. I would say "useless" answer, but each religion tends to spin a piece of how to deal with the dilemma. Either God isn't powerful in that way—didn't set up the possibility for solving our small human issues. Or God doesn't care about the hurt caused to humanity—because there's some other greater purpose we can't comprehend. Or that reality isn't as bad as we think it is—it's all an illusion. There's little way to reconcile these answers if you want to believe that your holy source has power, compassion, and intelligence. Good luck figuring that insight out. Greater theological minds than mine have gone round and round with that simple question: Why do bad things happen to good people? Or good things happen to awful people? We yearn for life to have a purpose and meaning that are defined by how pleasantly or unpleasantly we have it in this life. But that's not how life plays out. The unfairness of it all has been a point of consternation forever. How will we know if we're doing good or bad unless we feel definitive results from our actions? I can't tell you. I can recite all the platitudes, but ultimately if life is good or bad, the meaning of that will be obscure unless you do your own work to wake up to how *you* will put one foot in front of the other on your own spiritual journey.

TIME TO WAKE UP

Rock bottom. Are you there yet? If so, the good news is that an awakening might start to pull you up out of your hole. Grab the hand that's reaching for you and allow yourself to be held in divine goodness—no matter how bad it is.

Or are you just grousing more these days about those "other" people? Look inward, friend. Tell me what you see. Is the light in you bowing to the light in them? Then, Namaste. But if it's the asshole in you dismissing the asshole in them, then we call that in my house "na-masty" (rhymes with nasty). The mirror is a fabulously awful but effective place to receive some of the more difficult spiritual insights that wake us up.

Religious Community Requires Work

Though I've been talking about what it's like as an individual to participate in religious endeavors, religion is ultimately something you don't do alone. It is true that it varies, how much alone time or togetherness is expected among the different religions in practice. But it's a group activity—no getting around it. Even if you hole up in your hermitage and spend a year in silence, to be a religious activity you still need to have connection to others—be it through ancient texts, familiar prayers, or conversations that come to mind. You don't fly solo in a religious tradition.

But as with any community, the matter arises of understanding your relationship with the whole. Brené Brown explains this better than anyone else I know. She says she discovered that when you are thinking about any kind of social group, the opposite of belonging is fitting in. What she means is that many groups maintain their cohesiveness by everyone in the group conforming to certain norms and understandings: fitting in. If you mold yourself to be part of the group, that's fitting in, and it doesn't allow us to grow or change very much. But on the other hand, if you are in a group that practices belonging, each person is known and appreciated for bringing their whole selves to the enterprise. In groups like that, the participants grow alongside of each other, softening out the harder edges, and sharpening the insights and imaginations as they learn from each other. It's the harder way to be together. It can suck to be so vulnerable and possibly be rejected, but again, belonging feels like love in practice—because it is.

The faith that accompanies being grounded in a good religious tradition is beautiful and conducive to awakening because it gives you a picture of who you could be, but aren't yet. In an ideal world, religion gives humankind the structure and scaffolding that allows for questioning, diversity, and growth. It becomes, as my theology professor used to say, a living tradition of the dead, rather than a dead tradition among the living. Without a few of these guideposts of patterns, practices, and insights, you can feel adrift in an ocean of meaninglessness. If those rails are too constricting though, they can lead to a loss of faith, a disparaging of religion. That's when it's time to lose it or at least loosen it with deconstruction. Let's go there.

TIME TO WAKE UP

Love your neighbor. Love your neighbor. Love your neighbor. Be kind. Be kind. Be kind.

At the depth of every religious pattern, practice, or insight is a connection to other people. We are social animals with a divine destiny to manifest benevolence toward our fellow people, creatures, and planet. Good religion grounds us in this truth, and wakes us up so that we can start to become the kind of community that cares deeply about love and justice.

5

TEAR IT ALL APART
Losing My Religion

That's me in the corner. That's me in the spotlight. Losing my religion.

—Michael Stipe

WAKING UP TO YOUR OWN LIFE can be a bitch when it means getting honest with becoming your truest self. As you open your eyes to the interconnectedness of humankind, friends who haven't seen you in a while might look for the party animal you used to be and not like the reflective person you've now become. Or you may look back at what you used to believe about the immigrants taking our jobs or poor people needing to pull themselves up by their bootstraps and feel all cringey inside because you are becoming more accepting of the divine spark in everyone. Getting prepared to take on what you are meant to do in this world usually requires us to change because human growth requires change.

And change often means loss. If we have been conditioned either by a religion or by any other kind of systemic pressure to be one way, and we find ourselves at odds with that way, letting go of one strand of belief has the potential to unravel the whole garment—and many folks would simply rather not pull on that thread. It's too hard. And when the source of our thinking is imagined to be benevolent, the religious institution, the "life, liberty, and pursuit of happiness" promise of the state, then deconstruction of that thinking is likely to then also involve dismantling previously held understandings about the goodness of institutions you wanted to keep you safe or offer you comfort before any reconstruction is even possible. Awakenings that come through loss of trust can leave you truly hanging in a mess of *What do I think or know?* until clarity shines forth in a way you see with open eyes and accept with your opening mind. Seeing the world as it is, and then trying to love it into what it could be, is not for the faint of heart.

For there to be a collective renewal that allows us to step into the next epoch of our humanity's narrative—spoiler alert—it always gets really bad before it can turn and get better. Dark ages precede any renaissance. Wise guru in religion Phyllis Tickle is known for making the claim that Western Christianity every five hundred years or so collectively holds a rummage sale where we toss out the traditions and theologies that are no longer serving us, to make room for something new. Though

I am not particularly gifted when it comes to historical details, that claim also carries to spirituality patterns that repeat through history, because humans are culturally conditioned that way. Even our brains have literal ruts in them that keep us stuck in place until we are so dreadfully uncomfortable that we must make a change.

So when faith leaders are uninspiring ... when the rituals have become rote ... and when conformity and corruption stifle any hope in religious institutions for being spiritually refreshing, God will prepare an alternative way for the Spirit to breathe life into creation, humans included.

This kind of change doesn't only come on a large cultural level, but in our own lives. We will discover that the time has come to confront idolatry within our flawed institutions and rebuild the perceptions of what it means to be holy, kind, free, or compassionate. Though I do not imagine God as punishing us *for* our sins, I can fully see how we reap the natural consequences of our harmful actions, and I could personally attest to how selfish choices have blown up in my own life. I don't love this, but it makes sense. There are always innocent casualties affected by others' lust for power and greed for easy wealth. We cannot help but face up to our own madness that we have come to see as normal—the economic inequalities, the ravaging of the earth, the ugliness that fosters divisions, and the dis-ease that plagues us. The four horsemen of the Apocalypse ride again! That's the special surprise of Revelation. They are never not with us. End times are a recurring condition, not a finale. We must go through endings for there to be new beginnings.

And sometimes it feels as though those endings are going to destroy us. There's a reason some religious traditions name and claim a destroyer God. It makes perfect sense to me, the older and more jaded I get, that our ability to change our behavior in any meaningful way is slim. We just don't do it without a big slap to our egos to wake up.

Yes, we must wake up. As one awakens to spiritual truth and opens oneself to greater knowledge and awareness of themselves and of the world, the old ways will no longer make sense. The one awakened will feel alive in declaring the wrongness that they are starting to see. It doesn't make a lot of friends, but it is an identifier separating those who see from those who can't. But those whose eyes are opened to beliefs and practices that cause irreversible harm to our fellow human beings are constantly nudged to speak out about how such institutions have operated out of greed and lust and power. It's a part of the human narrative. And when eyes are opened, the pressure that a religion stuck in its own zealotry and certainty puts on us is seen for what it is. When that pressure can no longer hold us rigidly in our place, people begin to wake up to the incoherence of the system. Beware of a religion that comes off as too neat and tidy. The mess is where the action is. Loving the Divine and loving other people is never going to be as orderly as we think it could be. The aha moment of awakening is too great to deny, and those pressing for greater benefits for the whole seem a realm apart from those who just want everything to stay the same.

People who whine about human growth being the downfall of society's established norms aren't wrong. Because that's exactly what *is* happening. The world is changing and won't ever go back to the way it was. Really. Never.

Those who aren't coming to terms with this round of global awakening will get pissed and try for dear life to hold on to the old ways—as awful as they might be—because they are familiar. Many people will choose to complain about change and wish they could go back to their old reality.

Security holds a lot of weight. Transformation takes courage. Hold on, friends. That's when spiritual awakening goes into full prophetic mode. While mystics are known for finding comfort in the depths of their religion, it is the prophets who find their fervor and energy in taking religion to task and leading their people into the future reality.

Every prophet has a burr up their ass. Really, all of them. They may be uncomfortable with being asked to lead like Moses. They may be angry at God for sending them to Nineveh like Jonah. They may be giving their people bad news while weeping like Jeremiah, or foolishly talking about God's love until they get themselves killed like Jesus. That's just the dudes. The women who are called prophets are magnificent seers of the truth—wise and creative, but always wonderfully scandalous. Like Deborah leading her army to victory by sending the woman Jael to run a tent peg through the enemy commander's skull. Or like Mary Magdeline, apostle in her own right, talking back to Jesus like an equal. They are driven to speak their truth even if it will get them into trouble. Prophets dream dreams, stand in solidarity with those on the margins, loosen the chains of the captives, talk back to power, and undermine the status quo. However, powerful men want to quash the voices of prophets who might diminish their authority. And quietly obedient women who might not even get a footnote in history will do everything in their power to diminish women whose voices are too loud. The prophets are always the game-changers—and will not be silenced—even when power and propriety team up to shut them down. Prophetic men are the misunderstood spiritual geniuses, prophetic women are the wild and dangerous, and don't you just love that!

Be they old or young, male, female, or nonbinary, prophets come in a wide variety of every gender and cultural status, and they usually buck the expectations of anyone who wants to define authority under very gender-specific terms. Even in Scripture, they make a splash with who they are, and even more so, whom they are unafraid to challenge. And then, these awakened people will find ways of awakening more people.

It should be of no shock to us in difficult times that more and more voices are declaring the brokenness of religion. The prophets of old even quoted God saying that God hates and despises religion when it forgets its own purpose. God takes greater notice of an open heart than a filled stadium.

Why do we need all these prophetic, angry, sorrowful, depressing, deconstructing voices now? Because it's exactly in moments like this—out of chaos and despair—that we need to challenge the hell out of religion. We must remind ourselves that getting our relationships right matters more than doctrinal purity or ritualistic righteousness. Love is what matters. Yet, the white supremacist response to growing diversity is to use religion as an oppressive force. What we're seeing now is the mess, the set of clues all around us, that real change is possible—even if it is awful in the meantime.

These prophetic voices always sound like they are coming from the fringe and the margins, right? They are the activists and agitators. They boldly proclaim that Black lives matter, Indigenous lives matter, LGBTQ+ lives matter, women matter, non-Christian voices matter, poor lives matter—all because they speak the truth that those they advocate for have not always mattered "as much." The center, wherever power is, will benefit the most by quashing those voices. The powerful may do that in fascistic, authoritarian ways by means of cultural control, by manipulating legal codes, or by force. Or they may do it through hand-wringing around change. When the powerful claim that change will take too long or be impossible, then by default they can prevent their own top tier personal privilege and benefits from being lost to those they deem below their status. Power, be it of any political persuasion, never wants to befriend the edges of society—not really. Befriending the masses is only important for getting votes or selling products. But where power fails, the Spirit steps in; she always has. Love quietly walks into the room. Wisdom can be found wherever human suffering carries the mantle of hope for change and new possibilities.

You might be wondering if change is even possible, given the state of our world, and where we might be headed as a species. At different times, I wonder also, until I remember that the arc of history is long and trustworthily repetitive. However, I won't necessarily agree with those who say that the arc of history always bends toward justice. Sometimes the state of the day offers us a backlash of alarming proportions. We might be stuck with some generational payback for how we have wrecked creation and lost compassion for our neighbors. We will reap what has been sown, and unfortunately it hurts those with the least amount of power and resources first. But hold on. I don't believe we are heading toward all-out certain doom either. There are possibilities for awakening an ever-increasing number of people, and a time will come when that awakening reaches a tipping point where change must come and must be chosen. Awakening is being able to sustain a change of mind or heart—even when we are full of doubts.

Perhaps this is why the language of spirituality is now preferred to that of religion. Religion is seen as the codified fossil of ages past—stuck in keeping the masses content and the powerful in power rather than forging new pathways to the future. Through the statistics touting the rise of the "spiritual but not religious" and the nones, I perceive a desire to bring a broader range of emotion and nuance to our spiritual lives.

Here's where the hypocrisy of religion destroys itself. It promises the comfort of heaven at the price of ignoring our relationships in the here and now. It prioritizes the pleasure of its participants over the justified anger of those who see that the world isn't as it should be. Clergy temper their passion to please the least common denominator in their purple congregations—avoiding approaching anything that could be interpreted as politically red or blue. The religion of the sanctuary expects happy participants who keep their problems to themselves, even when groups like Alcoholics Anonymous are baring their souls in the basement. And so much of religion takes itself way, *way* too seriously. Geez, live a little, people. Even Jesus was called out for being a glutton and a drunkard.

So jettison the heavy baggage of religion and seek fresh air and a greater hope for the future. Loosen those halos and get to a place where we can seek together, get grounded together, build a future together.

We can't expect to always live on the bright side of life—or death, for that matter. We need to embrace the wholeness and vulnerability of being human. And it's going to take emotional, messy work. Those who are deconstructing religion now are vulnerably speaking more truth than those who are holding on to expectations of religion in stasis that somehow promises that they'll never be touched by all that affects humanity.

To lose the tight-assed religiosity without losing connection to each other, I think we need to be shaken from our places of comfort and turn toward the mess of life rather than seek a way out of it. There's a blessing I've been using in my teaching and preaching that I picked up from a conference preacher early in my ministry. It has become a guidepost for me. The startling nature of it seems to have a strong appeal.

Trying to find its origins, I've seen it called a Franciscan blessing or the fourfold Benedictine blessing, and I have noticed a multitude of ways people have adapted this prayer for their own use. Recently I discovered it has a contemporary author: Sister Ruth Marlene Fox, who wrote it in the 1980s when she was a chaplain for Catholic students at then Dickinson State College. But this is how I learned it:

> May God bless you with *discomfort* at easy answers, half-truths, and superficial relationships so that you will live deeply and from the heart.
>
> May God bless you with *anger* at injustice, oppression, and the exploitation of people so that you will work for justice, freedom, and peace.
>
> May God bless you with *tears* to shed for those who suffer from pain, rejection, starvation, and war so that you will reach out your hands to comfort them and turn their pain into joy.
>
> May God bless you with just enough *foolishness* to believe that you can make a difference in this old world so that you will do those things others say cannot be done.

Discomfort, anger, grief, and foolishness might not be what first come to mind when you think about a spiritual awakening, but all those circumstances certainly have the power to grab our attention and call for a response. When we realize that the world isn't as it should be, our first feelings might either rock or wreck our perception. Though religious patterns and practices themselves can teach us about living deeply and from the heart; working for justice, freedom and peace; comforting the afflicted; and making a difference in this old world, many people are not convinced that they have worked or will work on their own. We start to think that if God really loved the world and worked through our thoughts and prayers, a hell of a lot more should be better by now. We find ourselves upset, angry, and eager to give it all up to chance—or at least shaking our fist at the impotence of religion to accomplish anything.

Here's where I think exploring these blessings and allowing them to lead us away from the kind of religion that props up power and demands certitude can help. For those who have been steeped in religion, boldness is required to walk away from the security religion provides, even if your religion has been full of frustrations. Some folks wake up within their religious truth, others have to lose it to discover something richer outside of its crumbling fortresses. The conundrum of awakening has to do with such discernment—stay and fight, walk away and grow, listen to your heart, follow your gut. It's mostly intuitive and therefore a little amorphous. Yet I think that finding guides like Sister Ruth Fox who chart the course as they discovered it may give us what we need for the spark of awakening to lead us toward the depth of transformation.

In her case, Sister Ruth saw in graduating college students the need for a reckoning with the valleys—the lows, if you will—so she blessed them with a reliable pathway through the difficulties of discomfort, anger, grief, and foolishness.

If you find yourself deep in the trenches and losing your religion, consider her prayer a detailed map for where your spiritual journey might be headed: up and out of the places that hurt toward the transformation that can heal. The human power of transformation is knowing that we are not alone, and that others have been in similar entanglements before us—who may be blessed with a map, or a flashlight, or a hand to guide us to what's next.

May God Bless You with Discomfort

Oh my God. What if my parents were wrong? And my church was wrong? And my beliefs are all wrong?

Welcome to discomfort, that great change-maker.

If you were explicitly taught that there are always right answers and wrong answers on the test, and then you find out there is no test, or that the test is really about how well you get to know yourself and others, then *bam*: mind blown.

Perhaps the answers your religion gave you were too easy, too clear-cut, too much like the rules your parents seemed to make up to control you, rules you hated. When religious institutions cultivate compliant believers, those institutions benefit in money and power. They always have. Does your religion make money from giving you the answer to life, the universe, and everything (as it sees it)—or does it give from its bountiful resources toward the lofty goal of helping human beings exploring their deepest questions, no matter where that leads?

That the divine source is supremely powerful and generously benevolent: whatever else you believe about God or your gods, those two points are usually a set standard in religion. So when your God hates all the same people your religion does, then maybe your God isn't very big or very loving. So if your religion has a bunch of haters in it, you might be getting a few things skewed sideways. This hate is frequently justified by easy answers that religion uses to keep folks in check. *Those* people are criminal, or immoral, or otherwise less than. "How do we know?" you may ask your religious leaders. Well, they broke a commandment or didn't do exactly as our holy book requires. Simple, right?

If you are going to pursue the spiritual journey with diligence, the answers are going to become more complex and difficult. Where you once thought there was right or wrong, you will find a wide spectrum of possible outcomes and a not-so-clear set of moral certitudes. For many folks, this gets uncomfortable. It's why those teenage youth-group church kids get to college and feel like their religion is being destroyed by religious studies professors who are teaching from a historically critical perspective rather than from a faith bias. And why their parents then complain about college indoctrination and all those woke, liberal college types. But this kind of dismantling can lead to a more open concept of what religion could be. Knowledge allows folks to remove layers of small-minded beliefs to explore truth with a much wider lens.

It's also uncomfortable to let go of beliefs that are really only half-truths. Those hell-drenched, fear-inducing lessons preached with certainty are only part of the picture, tell only part of a story. We begin to imagine that the poor are just too lazy or that young people don't show the right amount of respect. But to get really uncomfortable, we must realize that poverty is built into the design. For the rich to be so rich, they have to take more than they need from somewhere. Most billionaires believe they deserve what they have in their bank accounts. That's a half-truth. Perhaps they were good with money or designed something a lot of people want. But to think that they deserve everything? Not so much. What if we looked at how they pay people who work for them—either personally or corporately? That may tell you how they value human life other than their own. And with young people—the youngest generation is often blamed for things that were simply handed off to them. We don't have a good imagination for understanding how our actions shape who the next generation is able to become. That takes complexity. To grow in depth is to imagine the full nature of what is true.

We've all experienced superficial relationships, the kind based solely on quid pro quo. The relationship is only as good as what I get out of it. When a church cultivates membership simply to add to the prestige of its number of souls saved or to gain more revenue in the offering plate, that's when religion uses its members for its own purposes rather than for the common good. There's a good reason these relationships feel icky to us—because they are. They don't speak to or from the heart. They are, in effect, heartless.

Those blessed by discomfort are those who move more intimately among people, who sense trustworthiness and the depth of a relationship in all its complexity. This kind of discomfort wakes us up to knowing our own selves and the divine principle much better.

TIME TO WAKE UP

What makes you uncomfortable? Start a list. Sister Ruth's blessing as a guide or begin your own. What are you changing because of your discomfort? If you cannot change that thing right now, how would you like to change it in the future? Allow that hope for change to begin to open your eyes.

May God Bless You with Anger

The anger that many religious folks espouse in our own time is a frivolous theological gymnastics that says God hates all the same people you do. If you can hate trans people, then maybe God does too. If you can hate Jews (or Muslims or Christians), maybe God does too. If you can hate immigrants, maybe God does too. If you can hate people of color, maybe God does too.

But the anger in the Bible—and there's plenty of it—is different.

The anger that God is slow to (in scriptural language) has a much deeper burn. God's prophets are routinely angered by injustice, oppression, and exploitation. Our anger would be better placed in confronting such issues in our own time. We have our work cut out for us, though, because these challenges to real anger *include us* rather than merely *excluding the other*.

We participate in injustices, known or unknown, by the words we say and the actions we take in our daily lives. We are likely to flourish in one aspect of our life or another because of some form of oppression. Maybe in the well-worn hierarchies of history, you have the culturally preferred skin color or gender identity. Maybe you were born into a powerful nationality or more well-to-do socioeconomic status. Maybe you have earned your way to being boss over one person or many. Maybe you find your authority in parenting children who must obey your commands or in being a bully in your friend group. Oppression comes in a variety of forms. We also exploit other people—knowingly or unknowingly. If you like the cheap prices of your favorite big-box store, or want to consume chocolate, or even drive your car, you most likely participate in exploitative business practices. That tomato on your sandwich—if it comes from a grocery store—maybe it was picked by migrant workers who are threatened with deportation if they don't work for a pittance in under-the-table pay.

Who makes God angry? We do. All of us. And I, for one, am grateful that God claims to be slow to anger, because if God were quick-tempered we'd all be goners. Deconstructing misplaced religious anger allows us to come back to the kind of real anger that all of us benefit from. Anger shouldn't be used to control other unique populations. Anger should be directed at the very things we ourselves do to create the animosity between people that destroys the social fabric of our lives.

True and righteous anger can lead us toward the kind of values that make for belonging: justice, freedom, and peace. We cannot experience any of these attributes alone. They are communal. I'm only as free as my neighbor is also free. Peace can only happen if aggressors like me, like you, let go of their aggression.

⏲
TIME TO WAKE UP

What makes you angry? Start your list. Get even more specific about the injustice that affects you personally or the oppression that makes your blood boil. Rather than take your outrage to the internet or into an argument that only makes you more frustrated, do something. What can you do to take the first step toward something different? If you can donate money to help others, great. Write to someone with the power to effect a change? Cool. Sometimes all you can do is the next load of laundry or go to work. How can that mundane task channel some of your anger productively? Allow your big feelings to wake you up even more.

May God Bless You with Tears

Here are things to cry about, for real. Poverty. Rejection. The innocent casualties of war. What if caring about the quality of our relationships is ultimately more important than practicing religious purity? Religion is easy if you don't care about hurting other people. But the blessing of tears calls us to compassion, to empathy, to making sure our tears flow freely so that we can weep with those who weep.

The argument has been made that God will always be present in the midst of our sorrow. Maybe that's true. Maybe it isn't. What I do know is that we need to accompany one another in the presence of human pain because it doesn't always feel like God is there. In fact, it may actually feel like God is wholly absent, where God is a fairy tale invented to try to assuage human misery. When we awaken to the plight of our neighbor, then we will be able to sit in the pain with others whether they are deeply faithful, casually religious, or the staunchest atheist out there.

TIME TO WAKE UP

What makes you sad? The sad-mad-glad trio are the list of feelings that most people can come up with—even when those big categories come with a great deal more nuance than that. Truly, what brings tears to your eyes? Grief, remorse, disappointment, pain, rejection? Get specific and find a way to lighten your burden.

Maybe you cry big, ugly tears of letting go. Maybe you talk to a friend. Maybe you collect the feelings in your body and metaphorically throw them into the pond near your house. Activity can help awaken us—especially when our religion has encouraged us to turn a blind eye to the pain caused in the quest for power. Whenever religion has benefitted from elevating the rich and turning away from the poor, or idealized men as having superiority over women, or endorsed colonialism to the ravaging of Indigenous populations or enslavement through a variety of forms, the necessary tears for those who became casualties of those horrors have been stopped from flowing. Let's unstop them together and find healing.

May God Bless You with Foolishness

Foolishness, my favorite part of this blessing. Get out there and do some crazy shit, not because God wants you to, but because it takes foolish people to challenge the status quo. If you see something breaking bad, please don't assume that all will go away because of your thoughts and prayers. Believe in God or don't—but don't believe for one second that God will take care of the world without your help. Yes, your help is required. You might choose to *believe* as though God is actively involved, but by all means, *act* as though God doesn't have one little finger to lift for the perils of humanity. If you want to see a difference in this old world, get out there and try something.

Sometimes trying something means losing our religion, learning to cry, to be foolish, to dare, to dare to say yes to awakening, to say yes to meeting the vulnerable in their pain—and to saying yes to being involved not only in belief but actions that bring about change. It takes some imagination and mess and willingness to look at our religion and our troubles from every single angle. But when you can get uncomfortable, get angry, build relationships, and imagine the world as you wish it could be, then you are awakening to action. Actions change beliefs, and a change in beliefs allows your spirit to transform and grow—even if you find yourself with far more doubt and uncertainty than you've ever had.

TIME TO WAKE UP

When have you acted the fool for a good cause? In one of the congregations that I served, I used this blessing a lot, so much so that I always saw people mouthing the words along with me, especially this end phrase. May God bless you with foolishness. What a delightfully scandalous blessing! Prince, legend who he was, might tell us, "Let's go crazy. Let's get nuts." It's time to be a fool so that we can get through this thing called life. Awakenings not only change us, they have the power to change the world when enough of us are willing to be foolish enough to show the world that a difference can be made.

6

SURVIVE THE DARK FOREST
Suffering Is a Feature, Not a Flaw

> *Remember if you want to make progress on the path and ascend to the places you have longed for, the important thing is not to think much but to love much, and so to do whatever best awakens you to love.*
>
> —Teresa of Ávila

TO REACH THE DESTINATION of your longing, eventually you will come up against the knowledge that your ego has to get out of the way for any new growth to happen. Early awakening experiences feel like you are being entrusted with something special, be it awe or responsibility or tradition.

And even if what you've awakened to and been entrusted with is criticizing the harms of religion, you come to feel righteous and purposeful, like your own action is needed in the realm of God's world. When you sense that you have been chosen to be a part of something bigger than yourself, you go out in search of it. Perhaps you found meaning in religion, or you found challenge in fighting the hypocrisy of religion. At the center of these adventures, there you are. You realized this is *your* journey, *your* spirituality, *your* growth. Right?

But awakening, though it comes to you and through you, can present an opening for even greater growth when you discover it isn't all about you. These lotus petals of awakening just keep opening and opening, don't they? But as the Buddhists say, "No mud, no lotus." The ongoing journey of awakening is going to slog through the mess, and this time take us through the proverbial dark forest. You already have guessed that you are not the center of the universe. But are you starting to realize that maybe you are barely even the center of your own story. Your ego, your identity, and our you-ness are the seeds that must fall to the ground and die to grow into the fullness of your own awakening. There may come a time when your sense of control and agency will be stripped away from you. Pain and suffering will overwhelm you. Your ineptitude for making things better will crush you. The night will turn dark. The forest will seem to have no way out. But even as the seed must push its way up through the dirt, another aspect of love's light will guide the way to the surface. This could come at you like a dark night of the soul, a midlife unraveling, a surprising grief, or your own existential crisis. Some of us are lucky enough to go through this cycle on repeat—no joke. Embrace the suckitude, maybe? Find companions who will walk alongside you and not be fool enough to say, "Well, everything happens for a reason."

Here's an example of how innocently the existential doom can creep up on you. Say you visit a museum and see a picture of the Milky Way galaxy with an arrow pointing to a speck on the edge of this one singular galaxy that is part of a vast universe made up of potentially two trillion galaxies. You learn that the speck is the massive object you know as the sun, an object nearly ninety-four million miles away from your home on planet Earth. And then you realize that you are but one of the eight billion people on this Earth, which is just an ordinary planet that orbits this ordinary sun in a random galaxy in the universe that may be within a multiverse and therefore even bigger than we have imagined. This may, shall we say, give you pause for a moment of existential breakdown. *What are human beings, O God, that you are mindful of them?* Psalm 8 asks a damn good question. At first when we awaken to this gift entrusted to us, we often look at ourselves as the gift rather than the gift itself as the gift. We think we are so tremendously, individually powerful. But how different am I really from just one of the ants in the anthill swarm or one of the objects in a galaxy tens of billions of light-years away?

Often what follows the ego response to a rude awakening that punches us in the gut is not the expected reminder that we are special or important or courageous. Instead, we're whacked with a sense of smallness and finitude. Feeling tiny and insignificant, *stick* with that feeling. That loss of self-centeredness is truly ripe for awakening. It's hard to allow it, to live into it, to let it take you where you might not want to go. Trust it anyway. That awareness that something that isn't us—and is far bigger than us—is at the center opens the gateway to new dimensions of spiritual awakening.

It's likely to give you a very different perspective on God once you have this very different perspective on you and your place in the world. And before it can lead to connection with the vast Oneness, there's of course the messiness: this awareness very well can drive you toward isolation, meaninglessness, and a long tango with how to possibly believe in a good God with all the world's suffering you are noticing everywhere. For many people, this awakening to our smallness in a vast universe, rather than just our you-ness, is a transition that often begins at midlife, which itself is a span of time, not a number. It may come across as an unraveling of your lived experience up until that point. All the "shoulds" and "supposed-tos" fall away. Even an awareness of God's presence that might have been strong before can dry up and feel like abandonment when you are hurting and alone. What do you do when the curiosity, comfort, or connection just isn't enough to get you through, and the immensity of the Divine seems disconnected from your personal suffering and the sheer magnitude of pain present in the world? The platitudes have all been said and dismissed as not helpful in the least. The door on hope has been quietly shut or loudly slammed. Now what?

You are noticing that, in fact, you are waking up—again, but waking up to what exactly? Because this doesn't feel good, or awesome, or emboldening. This could be an experience you'll be tempted to run from. You begin to realize that suffering, real human suffering, is not something you can avoid, and neither is it something to venerate. The miracle of consciousness renders both options null and void. Becoming open to the Oneness, enticed at first by the incredible beauty of all that is, you open yourself more fully—and now, try as you might, you cannot unsee all the ugliness that happens in the world, all the suffering that seems so unnecessary and vulgar.

Humans have tried all the things to mitigate such pain: reaching for comfort in certain experiences, mental numbing, or the cohesiveness of being in with your in-group. Up until now, perhaps even your religious faith offered a comfortable, snuggly blanket. But ultimately, these things are not enough to soothe the ache.

Maybe at first we tried to make sense of suffering, to wrestle meaning from meanness and truth from tyranny.

That doesn't work either. Sometimes there is no reason for what's happening, and the pain cannot be held at bay or explained away. Sometimes the anger stirred in us by the prophets to make things right leads us to a place of futility. We are unable to make the changes to heal the world's ills, and there's nothing left to do but accept the brokenness of the world as it is. This hurts. A lot. That's the stuff of depression, dark nights, and existential dread.

In come the mystics. An odd bunch. They always seem to drive toward pain, not away from it. It's why they seem so strange, often the outcasts within their established traditions even though they speak from the central tenets of what we might call old religion, and some today call perennial religion—the religion that always was and always will be, the religion that is ever entwined with the human experience. Mystics are the ones who see unity at the depths—that when it comes to the important truths and wisdom about life, we are far more alike than we are different. This scares the religious purists who can't let go of the absolute certainty of their own path, and it scares the skeptics who would rather toss out any connection to divinity when pain shows up, because who wants to worship a God that allows never-ending genocide, mass murder, and poverty?

Welcome to the dark forest, the point at which many folks turn around and go home. This may be a plot device for fiction writers, but in the spiritual realm it is merely the common reality. According to the mystics, though, suffering is a feature of this life, not a flaw. It is unavoidable, unless you are so out of touch as a narcissist or psychopath that you cannot feel either your own pain or the pain of others. But for most people, getting hurt or empathizing with the pain of others is a daily part of our existence. You can blame that on God. You can blame that on the greedy assholes who just don't seem to care about anything but themselves. You can blame it on fate that you either got or didn't get the dark forest you deserved. You can analyze all the triggers of traumatic experiences in hopes of avoiding them like potholes—but at some point, we all trip over something that is going to hurt us.

Before we can navigate the dark forest or discover ways to appreciate the dark night of the soul, we have to answer the messy question of theodicy—of awakening to a gift that shows us suffering and our smallness in the universe, that forces us to ask if our God(s) is/are so good, so loving, and so powerful, then why would he/she/they allow or create a human experience with such blatant horror happening in it?

All of a sudden, divine possibilities are cast as the monsters of the dark forest. Might as well oust them and try to deal with this shit on our own! Some atheists come to their atheism because they think any God must be monstrous to create a world with this much pain in it. But ask atheists what kind of God they don't believe in—and you'll likely find you don't believe in that God either (as Bill Richards would say).

Crushing humanity is not the name of the game here. The Living Spirit is not out to get us. The Source of our Being cannot be merely a fickle creature that dabbles in wars and pestilence, judging us for minor infractions, and toying with our emotional well-being until we wind up dead. If that turns out to be the case, count me in among the atheists!

Those who believe in a higher power will ultimately have unanswerable questions about why the world holds so much suffering, and these are questions you can't completely push to the side, atheist or not. Is that power benevolent in some potential long run we cannot see? Is the arc of humanity really bending toward justice, and if it is, for whom exactly? Is that power incapable of changing the dynamics that have been set in motion—all love, but not enough power to intervene? Or is God shaping us with such suffering as divine discipline—all power, but a kind of love we might find questionable? When God seems like both creator and destroyer, are those both legitimate interpretations of who God is? Where is that magic wand that would set things back to the "before," where beauty and innocence were all that was? What kind of God do I believe in exactly?

In addition to all those theodicy questions, a secondary question follows it when it comes to being awakened to suffering. Is it fair? In this life, can we anticipate that we will get exactly what we deserve? This Santa Claus theology gets the nice kids shiny new toys, good families, wealth, and success, while the naughty ones reckon with poverty, a lump of coal, and the pain of attributing their lot to their own sinfulness. This is a major feature of the prosperity gospel prominent among white evangelical Christian groups.

Testing that, the book of Job that shows up in the middle of the Bible confronts the "good person = happy life" theory. It ultimately cannot sufficiently answer the question, because there aren't cookie-cutter answers here either. We all know truly wonderful people who seem cursed with very shitty circumstances in their lives, and we have heard of a few billionaires who aren't the kind of people the gods would want to endorse.

For all the times I've thought that the consequences of a person's actions would be swift and exactly fit, for good or for ill, there are more times when the traumas of life absolutely do not make sense. Wonderful people die way too young, and old codgers maximize their secure prominent positions in the government to the detriment of others.

One day I was listening to James Finley's *Turning to the Mystics* podcast, and he offered something that helped me understand these questions. He reflected on two mystical paths that reveal how suffering might just be a feature of living a full-spectrum human life. Here I offer my own take on these directions.

Once you spiritually move beyond the allures of denial and self-soothing and offer a seat to your own sadness, the mystics can guide you deeper into your own pain and suffering as a path to transformation. One of these mystical paths through the dark forest is the path of trust in the face of unknowing. The other is the path of love in the face of suffering. Both paths help us meet the fears we face in the tough times of even our most difficult night.

As the prophets were split into human personifications of those with radically wild ideas and others with problematic disdain for the status quo, listening to the wisdom of the mystics stirs up aspects of divine attributes that seem to fall into a revolutionary yin and yang of masculine or feminine energies.

And while I use imagery of the feminine and masculine in order to understand the Great Mystery through the eyes of the mystics, that doesn't mean these traits or genders are rigid dichotomies—in the realm of spirituality or anywhere else. Holiness may be described as both male and female, yet it is neither male nor female. Holiness is a range and a perception. Religions have, of course, used immoveable interpretations of gender to alienate us from the fullness of ourselves, and to create hierarchies of human value. The mystics, however, bring masculine and feminine into balance in ways that are integrative and make sacred the whole of our being. And where the prophets speak bold truth to the outside world, the mystics concern themselves with how we understand our inner world—where we may feel more in touch with either our holy masculine or holy feminine selves, or perhaps some of both.

Whether you find yourself navigating the dark night or feeling exposed and vulnerable in broad daylight, becoming familiar with the mystics' sense of communion with the Divine takes us on an interior journey to understanding ourselves as those who receive gifts and are asked to honor them. They give us the language of what it is like to feel truly known or truly loved—no matter what hellscape might be going on all around us. They were not immune to history's darkest hours either. Again, oddities that they were and still are, the mystics wrote prolifically in exactly those eras of turmoil, as if to speak to not only their own but every apocalyptic age. If the prophets help us to change our world, the mystics help us learn how to change ourselves, even on days when change feels impossible.

The mystics of every religious tradition go deep and allow themselves to be changed by accepting life—suffering—as it is. They fully honor the present moment and the pain or relish in the joy of "now." They dance—their own spirit uniting with the fullness of the Spirit, which seems to put them in a realm all their own. But they are the teachers when it comes to the next level of understanding pain and suffering. They take our hands in theirs and look us in the eye and say things like, "All shall be well, and all shall be well, and all manner of things shall be well." Like an awakening, meeting them in that split second as we hear those words, we are inclined to believe them.

When our minds have been blown, our world shattered, and our hearts broken, the mystics seem to hold ways of being in the mess without the mess overcoming the delight of who we are as human beings. Mystics have these ways of receiving gifts and awakenings that make them special. They have navigated the depths and have insights and practices that they offer to us.

Knowing/Unknowing

Mystics help us meet our knowing—and our unknowing. I was awakened, rather uncomfortably, to understanding a mystical sense of knowing when I was one of two white participants in a class called Writing/Righting for the Resistance with Dr. Katie Geneva Cannon, a Black womanist theologian. In the class, she talked about the Black experience and the horrors and hardships of being

Black in America in every century since colonization. I asked Dr. Cannon, leading with my own sense of confoundment, "Look, I've seen white people become atheist when God doesn't answer their prayer for getting a good parking spot at the grocery store. *How* in the world do Black people not give up on a God that has not intervened through slavery, rape, violence, lynchings, and Jim Crow laws?" She gave me a *look* and said, "It's because we've always known who God is."

"Ohhhhh," I said, meeting her clarity with my own awakening.

White folks have long held the privilege—and it is a privilege—of simply believing in God, intellectually assenting to the notion of a higher power. Belief can come and go on a whim. Knowing goes deep into your bones. If you have been broken and bruised and denied your humanity, God is not just a pleasant thought, or a being you can control by going to church and saying your prayers. God is a force with the power to turn the world right side up. God is everything. Throughout Black churches in the United States, God is known. And God was heard speaking truth between the verses of the enslavers' Bible, even when the enslavers were perpetuating the lie that some humans were more valuable to God than others. That is knowing.

Carl Jung proposed something similar in his teaching about the collective unconscious. As one who studied the human mind, he was asked if he believed in God, and he said, "I don't believe in God. I know God." Knowing is the essence of human enlightenment. It is the bright light of truth. Knowing the light is not the same as factual knowledge. It is the depth of reciprocal knowing and being known, of not having to describe or defend, but just being held in that space of connection to the Oneness, the Unity, the Love that is, was, and always will be.

If knowing allows us to find solace in God's love and depth, then unknowing is what allows us to ponder the deep, unanswerable questions about the vastness of everything we cannot, do not, and will never fully know about God. It's praying in the way that *The Cloud of Unknowing* teaches, walking deeper and deeper into the fogginess of God until you become aware of your own smallness in the immensity of the universe. That's not a prayer method for everyone, but meditation that asks you to pray only with your breath is rather like it. You let go of thoughts, let them float on down the river, and simply trust that you are being held in a presence that is larger than you. Unknowing is being far less certain of what we know to be true, and feeling a deep and abiding truth in those mysteries we cannot ever fully and completely know.

When your awakening takes you on the mystical journey, curiosity circles back. But now it's a curiosity that acknowledges what you can know (the love of God), how much you don't know (as your trust in God grows, you realize that what you thought you knew five years ago is now inadequate), and never will be able to know (God is unknowable in God's entirety). When knowledge isn't relegated to certainty, it means that its growth has no end, and the beauty comes in allowing the divine maker to be trusted. It may mean that seeing the suffering around is seeing a suffering we can't heal, but we can meet that suffering, as this aspect of spiritual growth helps us grow exponentially in being in relationship to the heart of God.

This deep knowledge and relationship are part of the spiritual maturing process, as we learn in our knowing to find trust, and in our unknowing to be without judgment. Judgment derives its power and authority from certainty. It's about knowing what you know and being certain that you are right. But the knowing that comes from within frees us for constant growth and the ability to be moved and surprised by our surroundings. It also means trusting that your dot in the universe is meant to be trusted—that we receive the gift of awakening knowing (and now expecting) that the ego will get blown away by contemplating the vastness of all that is, and that we participate in that vastness.

Love/Suffering

Among the mystics who teach us how to make room for suffering are those who are adept at understanding suffering through the lens of love—especially the

Christian women mystics who startle us with their references to Jesus as Lover or as Mother. In their timeless writings we see how these women were sought out for their wisdom, for ways in which they knew suffering, and often nudged by both divine and human sources to write down what they knew—so that maybe we would later find truth in their words.

From experiences they frequently self-report as encounters with the Divine, the Spirit's gentle voice teaches us the profoundest meeting between love and suffering, something the writer of the Song of Songs said: "Love is stronger than death, passion more fierce than the grave" (8:6).

These women mystics who understood unknowing as the path to knowing, who knew how intimately suffering was related to—understood by—love, were also those who understood liminal cycles of birthing and dying. Those places of midwifing energy are filled with such a terrible and wonderful mingling of pain and grief and love and abundance. They knew that, in order to enter the spiritual dark forest with others who were in those spiritually tenuous places, they needed to become familiar with the dark. But it's not always clear what you are going to get when you enter the unknown. This darkness that was so familiar to them and sometimes not as familiar to us is not meant to inspire fear—but rather trust or love. We learn to love what we cannot completely see.

One such mystic, Julian of Norwich, is probably best known by her statement, "All shall be well, and all shall be well, and all manner of things shall be well." At first glance, this seems like an empty platitude. How could she possibly be so naïve about the world? No, Julian, everything is not well, thank you very much. It's suffering all day, every day. Don't be such a Pollyanna. But if you read more of Julian than just this quote, you will begin to understand that she had a huge reckoning with the suffering in her own life, and it was during an intense period of her own pain that she felt Jesus whisper those words in her ear. Rather than dismiss that as a fever dream, she articulated that experience as a means for trusting completely in the Divine anytime we experience human suffering. Our pain does not get the last word—ever.

The mystics are our balance in an imbalanced world. Truth and love go together. Righteousness and justice and peace go together. Dark and light flow together. Knowing and unknowing. Masculine and feminine. Suffering and love. The mystics show us that embracing the diversity in our humanity, facing both suffering and love, is to meet the Holy One in divine unity.

Even as we suffer in the now and not yet of it all, we are given glimpses of these paradoxical truths, and they are hard to retain. Recall those moments of encounter or awakening, a particularly awe-inspiring spiritual experience—and you may feel like you can't hold onto that bliss or awe. But in that place of unknowing, of letting go of our certainty, we may find that the nature of heaven is holding on to us. The mystics tell us so: "All shall be well."

What the Mystics Knew about Surviving the Dark Forest

No, there's absolutely no way to avoid suffering in this world, but now you know that you can meet this suffering with love. And when you do, you can begin to see suffering—the unknowing, the dark wood—as merely a feature and not a terrible flaw of human existence. For those times, I hope you find these gathered nuggets of truth culled from the mystics to be a light on your path.

TIME TO WAKE UP

What do the mystics teach us? How do you encounter these understandings in your own life?

About unknowing:

Most outcomes are not in your control.
   Quit worrying about what you cannot change.
The more you know, the less you know. You know?
   Prefer to be humble and grow rather than being braggadocious and right.

Faith is about trust, not certainty.

> *There are many paths to holiness, not just yours.*

The problem isn't fear, it's the rigidity that comes alongside being afraid.

> *Something new is being born, do you not perceive it?*

About love and suffering:

Love is stronger than death.

> *Compassion is always our greatest virtue, even when it costs us dearly.*

Life is hard, but grace abounds (Dr. Douglas Ottati).

> *All shall be well (Julian of Norwich).*

God is good—All the time. All the time—God is good.

> *Blessed are the poor, meek, and persecuted.*

Those who are humble will be exalted.

What Kind of Universe Will You Have?

The mystics who know deeply, who understand suffering and love, ultimately prepare us to believe in a benevolent universe, even when it seems to be strikingly the opposite. They can be perceived as wise beyond comparison or daft beyond belief. You get to decide for yourself. And as your awakening begins to torch your ego and leaves you reeling to the reality of your smallness in the universe, you just might be on the path of wise and daft beyond belief.

Having companions in your time of lament and depression and the dark forest is crucial—whether they are the consolation of the ancient writings of the mystics or friends who offer you companionship. Whether you believe that suffering is transformative or that it is just horrible luck maybe isn't the most important thing. What does matter is that you have received and accepted this invitation to your own life: don't try to cover it up or make it go away. The suffering will stay in its suckitude until you reckon with it and give it space to heave its sighs and cause its share of troubles. The mystics invite you to your own life of suffering and love. Like in Rumi's poem about the guest house, in which you invite *everything* about your experience in—good or bad—and let it do what it came to do in the present moment: "Be grateful for whatever comes," the poem says, "Because each has been sent, / As a guide from beyond." Then you can rage or heal or grieve or do what you need to do to experience your own personal, intimate connection to the vastness of all that is, was, and ever will be.

7

LET IT GO
Unraveling the Known, Discovering Mystery

I see skies of blue and clouds of white
The bright blessed day
The dark sacred night
And I think to myself
What a wonderful world

—George David Weiss and Bob Thiele

WAS IT CURIOSITY? Was I chosen by God or by my demographic? Did all previous roads lead to this?

Call it fate. Call it luck. Call it destiny. Call it providence.

Call it the algorithm that led me to an application process.

With gratitude to any or all of the unseen forces setting the itinerary for me, I was gifted a trip on the bullet train to the interior journey, what the late Roland Griffiths dubbed the "crash course" in spiritual awakening.

In the current energy motivating a resurgence of research into psychedelics—sometimes called "entheogens," for their ability to help some people see God or experience spiritual depths—in 2018, I was among those selected to participate in a study of spiritual practitioners at the Johns Hopkins Center for Psychedelic and Consciousness Research in Baltimore, Maryland.

Headed by the gentle spirit of researcher Roland Griffiths, the premise of the study was to document the effects of significant (read "heroic") doses of psilocybin (the active drug in magic mushrooms) on individuals considered established leaders in their respective religious traditions, those familiar with the vocabulary of spirituality but naïve when it came to use of psychedelics. I fit that profile. And I was curious enough in my own spiritual journey to want to know more. My understanding of the goal of the study was to learn if the alternative state of consciousness precipitated by the effects of the drug coincided with and confirmed the nature of mystical experiences. Are they the same, different, or somewhere in between? For me, taking psilocybin was tremendously powerful and unusual, more impactful spiritually than times I've felt God's closeness in prayer or meditation—and yet remarkably similar to those times I've had full-blown mystical experiences occur naturally (if "natural" is the right word). There was that bathroom conversation in Philadelphia that came out of the blue, and another opening that came during a retreat where I intentionally was seeking divine direction for my life.

I will leave it up to the researchers to publish their own findings on the study participants, both there and in other similar studies happening around the world. I was simply grateful for the opportunity to be a data point in a rather profound way. My hope is that these studies will continue to open conversations about the therapeutic and spiritual use of psychedelics. But make no mistake: these potent compounds create alternative states of consciousness.[1] Such power is not something to be trifled with. Some people may have medical or psychological conditions or prescription contraindications where use of these compounds may not be beneficial. Nor are they for every spiritual seeker. Used wisely and with care, I believe that some, however, may sense a healing and wholeness that can come from such an experience, but only if it makes sense within the context of the person's

---

[1] Generally speaking, and with limited exceptions for peyote and ayahuasca, most psychoactive plants and fungi are illegal to possess or consume under the federal Controlled Substances Act. And while some states and municipalities have decriminalized psychoactive plants and fungi, it is nonetheless important to fully understand the limitations of local government action in order to properly appreciate your legal exposure and personal risk. The same holds true for religious exercise with psychedelics, which may be protected under the First Amendment and Religious Freedom Restoration Act. Exercise due diligence, including consulting legal counsel if necessary, prior to engaging in the use of psychedelics.

own spiritual journey and health journey. My suspicion is that, first, one must feel ready for the journey it can take you on. Not everyone will be drawn to it as I was. Earlier in the book I reviewed some of the ways—and there are plenty!—to get mystical. As a practical matter, there are a whole range of concerns to consider: from safe settings, to who might fairly profit from their use, and their legality. And if and when mushrooms or any other psychedelics become differently regulated for either therapeutic or religious use, we should consider how best to honor and show gratitude to the Indigenous communities who discovered the medicinal value of these plants and compounds and who understand them within the sacred nature of their own rituals. But when it comes to the psychedelic adventure's potential for spiritual awakening, while I cannot speak for anyone else, I can attest to the experience I know: my own.

A bit of sound advice is given by all experienced trip-sitters: no matter what you encounter in a different state of mind, be curious about it and let go. Surrender. Fighting whatever surfaces is what gets folks into trouble. See a dragon? Look it in the eye and ask it what it came to teach you.

The cross-stitched throw-pillow instruction "Let go and let God," as trite as it may sound, is solid advice. For those awakened to new insight and choosing a change of path, that advice will likely resonate. My journey in letting go began long before I knew about the study, and I daresay it will continue to shape my life until I journey beyond this earthly existence. The spiritual life is a setup from the beginning. The more we learn, the less we know. And the less we know, the more creative our questions can become. In that openness, curiosity, and yes-ness, the luminescence in all that is begins to glow within. Everything begins to feel connected, purposeful, and just plain right. The story arc of your life begins to make sense, even when outwardly it looks like it doesn't. The story is less about the life you thought you could control and more about the life that continues to be a gift to you: the life God lives through us because we live in God.

Mystical experiences frequently defy the language that we bring to them. And as with all the chapters preceding this one, the realm of spiritual, religious, and even mystical exploration will be unique for each person. How awesome is that? Yet I also believe that these awakenings, from subtle growth over time to amazing transformations that happen in an awe-inspiring moment, share some common characteristics.

The curiosity, chosen-ness, faith, love, and suffering that I have described in previous chapters as nuances of the spiritual journey were all fully present and fully illuminated as I spent six hours tripping in a room set to be pleasant but not too distracting alongside my two trip advisers, mental health professionals who cared for me and my safety as I ingested my prepared psilocybin capsule and let it do its thing.

As I said, one of the qualifications of the study was a participant's not having any experimentation with psychedelics prior to the study. The background research for the study was thorough. I answered a barrage of mental health and spiritual experience questions, had a physical, was directed to seek medical attention for my high blood pressure in order to proceed safely, and spent several lengthy counseling sessions with Bill Richards, one of the foremost expert psychologists in this field, before my day came to be truly tested.

As I prepared for my psilocybin experience, I even practiced listening to parts of the official playlist, headphones on and with my eyes covered lying on the couch to simulate the bodily feeling of being relaxed in the space. That kind of research setting and intense commitment to the length of time and concern for detail that a scientific study takes might not be for everyone. There are other ways to have a psychedelic experience, and both the care for creating a safe environment and the guides themselves will vary in true qualification and responsibility to holding the space for the journeying participants. Knowing what to expect and trusting my guides were important to me. In turn, their own commitment to responsible administration, my safety, and follow-up was important for them. I found it comforting to feel so prepared—and to know that after the experience, Bill and my other guide, Claudia

Turnbull, would continue to follow up with me for eighteen months or longer, as they even now continue to answer my emails.

When the day for my trip came, I put on comfortable clothes and had my spouse drive me to the drab building on the campus of the Johns Hopkins medical facilities. In the space, I relaxed, I prayed, and I took the pill prepared just for me with some water from a chalice. There was art and music and a sense of sacred community created by all who had taken this journey ahead of me. Then, as the roller coaster inched up the hill to the point where there were no more choices to be made, I was on the ride with no way off—until it was over.

James Finley, clinical psychologist and former Trappist monk, well known for his embrace of the mystical realms, describes mystical rapture as that event after which you are never the same. Teresa of Ávila notes that it has a quality of absorption. John of Patmos writes down the incredible visions that became the biblical book of Revelation. Mystical rapture may or may not be an induced experience. The desert mothers and fathers experienced God through ascetic practices. Some mystics prayed for the fevers or disease so that they could see Christ. Those who have practiced the art of meditation know the peace that comes from oneness. And those who foraged mushrooms or licked toads or mixed certain plant roots were rewarded with a pathway to a state of consciousness one can experience for a few minutes of jetting into the stratosphere, or several hours of wrangling with the depths of anything and everything your mind decides to imagine.

When the intensity of the trip was subsiding, Roland Griffiths entered the comfortable couch room and started asking me the follow-up questions. One of the first was, "Did you have fun?" Fun? I laughed and laughed and laughed. And finally answered, "No, not at all, that sucked." What I realized as I started journaling almost immediately with my brain firing as it had never fired before was that it sucked in the most profound and wonderful way that I could have imagined.

Was it fun? Was it terrifying? Was it both simultaneously?

To describe the experience is to try and make a timeline out of it, but there is no solid timeline to this kind of adventure. For those of you who are fans of the television series *The Good Place*: "Yes, Chidi—everyone here knows about the time knife." My brain was fully active with the development of thought and imagination but not in any logical or sequential kind of way. It was like experiencing everything, everywhere, all at once (my nod to the kind of multiverse experience explored in the movie bearing that title).

So rather than try to explain what can neither be written in words or even be captured fully with cinematic possibilities, it might help to simply make some connections to spiritual themes common both to my six hours on the couch and the rest of my life's journey. I might add that the advice for letting go applies equally well to both.

Fear

Even though my preparation had been thorough, there was a real fear associated with swallowing that psilocybin capsule. A teenager in the era of Nancy Reagan's "Just Say No" campaign, I complied with the command. But in recent years, as I read and studied, I learned some valuable information that put Nancy's propaganda as an all-or-nothing proposition into question. The compound I would be ingesting was safe (within the parameters of my medical release to proceed) and nonaddictive (contrary to the claims during my teen years led me to believe). But the propaganda spoke to the risks: the unknown is still scary.

So, as with all magnificent spiritual experiences, I was hoping that some angelic presence would show up and tell me, "Don't be afraid." Those angels say that for a reason, don't they? In the counseling sessions that led up to the event, I had the benefit of exploring what my fears might be. But in the actual moments, they showed themselves—again—as fears tend to do. What if there was bodily discomfort, and I wanted off the ride after I was already strapped into my seat? I might throw up, or lose my mind, or embarrass myself, or who knows what? What if my blood pressure soared, and they needed to rush me to the hospital to get me out of the experience quickly? I assumed those risks by staying in the study. What if it was all too much and I lost my faith or felt overwhelmingly terrified?

Spiritually I knew I would be changed, and I wasn't quite sure how. That's dangerous, considering that up until the time of this study I had made my living as a member of the clergy.

Allowing oneself to truly be spiritually open to whatever possible God-experience you might have is frightening—or at least it should be. To be guided in such an experience requires a whole lot of trust. In certain intense circumstances, openness to the Spirit can feel like a push more than gentle encouragement. Perhaps it's better to meet our experiences with a few doubts, a healthy dose of skepticism, and humility. Who am I to think that God is directing my steps? Well, if we choose to communicate to God with our prayer and longing, maybe we do sometimes get the flash of beauty or moment of terror that allows us to experience God's choosing to be with us as well. It's holy ground, folks. Take off your sandals and let it be.

Luckily, I was traveling with those who had already been through the landscape I was about to experience. Though I knew little of what to expect, my guides were ready to be supportive of my journey. When opening the door to the unknown—even when you ultimately take that walk alone—it's helpful to have wise and trained professionals who are companions encouraging you to let go of your preconceived notions and engage the experience in a fresh way.

All of us have our fears and trepidations that prevent us from acting in certain ways. Some fears are natural, and others maybe were taught to us by those trying to keep us safe. Say, for example, someone were to tell me that I could have had the same amazing spiritual awakening by stepping out of a perfectly good airplane with a parachute strapped to my back. My answer would be a solid "Absolutely not" and "Never ask me that again." Just because I was brave enough to do this one thing doesn't mean that I would sign up for just anything. God knows this about each of us. My "This sounds potentially life-changing" could be your "Oh, hell no."

But part of the awakening experience is to do something that will likely make you pee your pants a little. Look the dragon in the eye. Enter the dark cave. Speak even though your voice shakes. Shut up and listen when your friend is telling you something heartbreaking. Perhaps you will wrestle with God all night and receive a blessing in the morning.

Embodiment

We live and move in our bodies. Most of the time, we assume that the narrator or movie clips that live inside of our heads are us. Dualist Western thought has always split the two—mind and body. The mind was thought to be the superior realm, and the body just a meat sack. But we human beings are somehow an integrated *both*.

Letting go of the typically assumed way of being in my body with my mind (maybe) in control of things seemed, well, different under the influence of psilocybin. I could feel music as though it were being played through me. The dimensional way that I normally see was altered and seemed more real than before. It's kind of like imagining what it would be like to see, smell, and taste through your dog's eyes, nose, and mouth. It was a complete and utter perspective shift.

Experiencing a perspective shift can come from anywhere, anytime. In my younger years, my perspective shifted in a conference center bathroom in the early morning in an unfamiliar city, so you never truly know. But we can practice letting go of our usual ways of seeing as well. You can imagine being born into different circumstances, a different socioeconomic status, different skin color, different gender, different nationality. Walking in someone else's shoes changes us. Although you can't entirely walk in someone else's shoes, trying to see different perspectives and different life circumstances opens us up to other ways of being in the world. You can experience new places and new people through travel to a culture unlike your own or take on a challenge for which you feel totally unprepared. The pilgrimage, which is an intentional spiritual practice for many, means taking your body with all of your experiences and walking them around on unfamiliar ground. It breaks you out of your normal bodily experience and offers you a spiritual chance to respond—differently—to any changes you see, hear, or feel.

Letting go of your identity just enough to experience deeper empathy for others enables spiritual openness. You begin to see that even though you know God loves you, God also loves your neighbor who's a jerk and the enemy you might not want to kill anymore. To take a different road, see things differently, visit a new land, meet a new culture, have a new experience—all can bring us also to those interior places where we can see or hear differently.

Emotion

What is it like to utterly let go of your emotional filter? I was taught through the era of my upbringing that it's never a good idea to be fully and unashamedly expressive of my feelings. Don't cry. Don't yell. Don't make a fuss. Don't be so joyful. Tamp that shit down! And for the most part, I do think it's necessary to read the room and gauge my reactions according to how safe I am or how professional I need to be. So it might not come as a surprise that with the filter blown by the psilocybin, a whole floodgate let loose. I have never let myself grieve like I grieved. I have never expressed anger as I was able to express anger. Both came as a surprise as well as a catharsis.

Afterward, Bill mentioned that it's not uncommon for the clergy in the study to have, as he put it, some "unexpressed anger" that comes out during the sessions with spiritual leader participants. When you have been fully conditioned not only to hold on to your own emotions but to welcome in and be a repository for the emotions of others, that shit piles up. We all need those safe places where we can express our humanity unhindered and unfiltered and to its fullest possible extent.

Unfortunately, social media has become a terrible outlet for unfiltered emotion of a different kind. But it results not in catharsis but an outrage that keeps people scrolling, expressing feelings from behind the protective anonymity of a screen name with relatively few if any visible consequences for their behaviors. It may discharge the feeling at the time, but doesn't allow for a more productive and interactive outcome to whatever is causing the anger in the first place. To let go in this way is not spiritually helpful or healthy. It's just a way to hurt others with your own pain.

To experience spiritual well-being through the expression of our emotions requires that we acknowledge the interconnectedness of humanity—a sense that what makes me sad, angry, or joyful are similar to what might make you sad, angry, or joyful. The emotions I accessed during this journey were like that—on the level of full human consciousness, not just my own thoughts and opinions run amok. In that state of being it was as though I could feel how God feels—with all our grief, pain, and joy. I liken it to the ability of the prophets to speak for God, to articulate with certainty how God feels when we seek justice and love kindness and walk with gentleness, or how God feels when we go way off target in truly seeing and caring for one another.

When it comes to experiencing the anger and grief that accompany true compassion, I wonder, *Can I, will I, truly sit with the pain, allowing it to reach my heart and soul?* Letting go of how I am supposed to show my feelings so that I can actually feel my feelings—well, that's the prescription for a lifetime of spiritual practice right there. Comparatively, disengagement is a piece of cake.

I was expressly taught how to be a so-called nonanxious presence as a spiritual leader. Keep those feelings covered up or on the down low. It makes sense to regulate my own anxieties in order to help a friend or congregant confront and deal with their own experiences of worry and dread. Yet we all need to do our own work in letting our true feelings find expressions that aren't harmful to others.

Among other things, God might be defined as the ultimate receiver of our human emotions, right? Prayer to our holy source includes lament, frustration, joy, gratitude, and all the other biggies of the emotional world—and we don't know quite what to do with that. Is God the unmoved mover? The wrathful judge who lets no minute grievance go unpunished? Impotent to do anything about our condition as humans? Loving but powerless? Where does God fit in?

While that awakening at dawn in that Philadelphia bathroom was significant and became a call for the change that led me to seminary, awakenings are like waves. When we say yes and stay open, more may come. And now, after this experience, something deepened. I now know God as feeling all our grief, all our pain, all our joy, all our everything. In my tradition, God is incarnate in a human, Jesus. But maybe incarnation is even larger than that—it's the whole of human and divine consciousness connected through these pathways where we experience a whole range of thoughts, emotions, and just be-ing as a real letting-go.

The Death/Rebirth Spiral

Like on cigarette packaging, perhaps there should be an all-caps warning label that comes with taking psychedelics. "WARNING: On this ride, you might experience death, or birth, or be one of the ones who gets the full spinny ride with birth, life, death, and rebirth coming around and around and around again."

Lucky me. I got the carnival-ride version of this trip—me, who won't ride anything faster than the merry-go-round at actual theme parks.

The pre-session advice I was given was that if death shows up, go ahead and die. If you think you might go crazy, go crazy. If you are birthing, breathe into those contractions. Lean into it. Let it happen. On this trip, I birthed, I died, I asked to be buried. I went down to the depths and came through glowing on the other side. It was a true roller coaster that went both higher and lower than I could have imagined.

For anyone seriously afraid of change or new ideas or death, this particular drug experience might not be for you. It's not a simple feel-good buzz. Smoke some (now in more places legal) cannabis, have a drink, or eat some carbs or sugar if you want a relaxing experience. If you need hype—have an espresso. Psilocybin and the mushrooms that produce it are known as "the teacher" for a reason. They can offer you the lessons you didn't know you needed, and then some.

Like looking at the "you are here" pictures of our planet's smallness in the breadth of the universe, with the psilocybin compound, there's a good chance that individual selfhood will die to give way to universal connectedness. Not just feel like loss of identity or death: death. Given that my scheduled experience occurred the week after I had led my congregation through the Christian Holy Week—recounting Jesus's Last Supper with his disciples, his arrest, trial, persecution, death, and resurrection—it was not surprising to me that multiple themes from Jesus's Passion showed up during my psilocybin trip.

As the use of psilocybin and other psychedelics becomes more widely accepted through approvals for mental health use or religious ceremony, or simply through decriminalization, I strongly recommend that anyone considering this path have prepared, professional, responsible trip-sitters. Seek mental health professionals who can calm you or refocus your attention if you become afraid—or as in my case, a little too enthusiastic. At one point I jumped off the couch, rather clumsily, much to the surprise of my trip-sitters. This was an anomaly from their usual sessions. The old drug-scare propaganda of my youth used to portray taking psychedelics as "losing your mind" and doing dangerous things. This was not that. The setting I was in couldn't have been more safe and serene. Much thought and detail had gone into making it that way. But at one point in the session, I wanted to physically dive into a painting in the room, and I expressed that in a physical way rather than just metaphorical. So in my own way of making it weird, I bumped my head on a coffee table and spent some time on the floor—no worse than any injury I could have gotten tripping over something in the dark in my own home. Nevertheless, what that fumble did was instigate the feeling that I was dying. I allowed it. I "died" into the arms of one of my guides, and as I did, the transformation I felt was magnificent. It set the scene for me to melt into my own death being held by Mary, just like Michaelangelo's marble sculpture—the *Pieta*—a sculpture I had the privilege to see during another spiritually rich time in my life.

This experience gave me deep gratitude for my own existence, and for the connectedness I share with all people, understanding that no one was better than me or lesser than me. It ultimately made me feel more gentle and more kind. It made me envision my guides as if they were angels, and it made me less afraid of what death is going to be like when my own earthly time is complete.

This was not the only death that I encountered during my experience, though it was probably the most profound. Just like I learned the religious pattern of birth, life, death, and rebirth through my church experience, my entheogen experience led me to know the same pattern in a very personal and up-close kind of way. I felt it in my very being. I felt it with Jesus, and I felt it as the key to a pattern available to humankind in so many of the world's religions.

Letting go—even of the significance of my own life—for the wonder and miracle of the whole is an awakening of significant proportions recognized by a whole range of religious traditions. Thinking back to surrender, resurrection, deliverance, and so on, I saw the whole as greater than the part I play in it and felt that as a wonderful gift.

Tradition

Almost simultaneously with noting the possibility of my own death, I began an intimate journey of noticing and an openness to an interweaving of religious truths. Being someone who has been trained in and led life along a particular version of the Christian narrative for decades, one might think that the Christian pathway is rutted so deeply in my mind as to be nonnegotiable. Turns out—not so much.

I experienced this trip immediately after the Easter cycle in my own tradition, and on that floor I found myself reliving the story of Jesus's Passion as if it were happening to me personally. Then the mood and music shifted where I encountered what seemed to be a Hindu expression of divine destruction (Shiva or Kali energy) and felt the presence of the open-handed Buddha. I felt what it was like to have the mouth of a prophet and the joy of dancing with the Spirit. I could go deep and still connect across a broad range of traditions, stories, and belief systems. I touched the incredible depth of holiness in my own tradition and discovered that it was tied to any and all truth discoverable in other expressions of God's being.

This is the holy ground, or perhaps the holy grounding. When connecting with the consciousness that unites us, the depth of God is present and numinous. Whatever name one chooses for the Divine, in this state of mind there weren't competing traditions, not even really differing traditions, just holiness. Just connection. In mystical and psychedelic adventures this is called the "unitive consciousness." Even atheists who have had such experiences will say that they "met God" even if they do not let go of their belief that God doesn't exist.

Bliss

You can't capture ecstasy or keep beauty locked up in a jar. I experienced bliss in the journey as color and light, but far more than those. It wasn't just happiness. It was profound joy that left room for nothing else. And even in that experience, I knew I couldn't stay there. I had to let go of that, too.

Maybe that's how it ought to be: we keep striving for it, circling back to it. The human longing for bliss—which I understood as heaven or paradise—is very real. We want to know such fullness. We are drawn to it because we have experienced its lack or its degradation in this world.

As the effects of tripping began to subside, I starting to feel back in my body the wonder, joy, and security that lingered. The terror passed and what persisted was the sense of life as a gift in a kind of glow that is difficult to describe. That's an awakening for you—with or without psilocybin. True awakenings are classified as being "difficult to put into words." Amen to that.

Confirmation

Waking up, the trueness of my truth felt truer than it ever had. Then in the short-term integration of my experience, it felt like everything I thought I knew before was speculation. To not just believe but to *know*, to feel experiential firsthand knowledge of holiness is exquisite and mind-bending and awe inspiring. And still a bit terrifying. To enter the holy of holies is a big deal. It always has been.

This shift from speculation and belief about to *knowing* gave me new eyes for interpreting Scripture, and preaching, and praying—corporately and personally. I felt closer than ever before to the Ground of my Being. And yet, as you might imagine, my religious training felt like it had been scrambled in the process. Was I still a Presbyterian pastor—with all the trappings and expectations of that role? I sought spiritual counsel and theological grounding from a small number of people in my circle of friends. They heard me question and probe—and offered compassion and curiosity, the best gifts I could have asked for. My congregation began telling me how, even more now, they felt inspired by my preaching and by my counsel. It turns out that having a pastor more attuned to the spiritual realm supported congregants through deepening insight and care.

I was so glad that I submitted my name for the study, drove back and forth to Baltimore, and swallowed a pill that gave me such a profound spiritual experience. What I decided not to do was take the second journey—one that they later told me would have increased the dose in the rubrics of the experiment. Maybe that would have taken me even further on the journey—though I don't know how. What I do know is I was led to be there. I was changed. And that change continues to affect others.

Catharsis

When I think of how best to describe my journey with psilocybin, it is an *exquisite wound* for which I will be forever grateful. Awakenings suck. That was the title of the after-report I sent to my guides. Bill Richards said to me after that Huston Smith was known for saying, "Ecstasy [the feeling of awe, not the drug] is not fun." Can confirm.

My most profound spiritual experiences have been varied and yet hold similar characteristics. I have felt called and confirmed, challenged and connected. The pain included in them has been meaningful, purposeful—and yet the lightness of being that followed was always surprising.

In the experience of truly and fully letting go of my small self as I connected with the Greater Mystery, I learned some things. Wherever you are on the spiritual journey of awakening and meeting the Mystery, these may also be insights you learn as well.

TIME TO WAKE UP

Reflection on Letting Go

I am unique and special in the particularity of who I am. The me that is me—matters.

I am one with everyone and everything else. The me that is me—is no more important and no less important than any other being.

I can be brave.
I can be kind.
I know God. And God knows me.

8

ANSWER THE CALL
Waking Up Every Day

We must let go of the life we have planned,
so as to accept the one that is waiting for us.

—Joseph Campbell

BUMPER-STICKER THEOLOGY CLAIMS that "God is my co-pilot" for a reason: that pesky ego wants us to feel as though we are fully in control of our own destinies, right? I mean, who really wants to have God in the driver's seat of their lives? We want to believe *we are the pilot.* The choice-maker. It's my life and I earned it—good or bad. If I'm successful, wealthy, and good-looking. that's because I did exactly what was right in my life. And if I'm stressed out, poor, and haggard from my own poor choices, I must have had that coming too.

Joseph Campbell, known for studying the impactful stories of spiritual journeys from a multitude of religious traditions, came to a different conclusion. The planned and procured life is a falsehood. It can be let go, tossed aside, fully and functionally dismissed, because the real life, the authentic life is the one that has been designed specifically for us and that is waiting for us—if we were to only allow it to happen. "We must let go of the life we have planned," he wrote, "so as to accept the one that is waiting for us." That's a blow to my personal sense of control.

What kind of crazy bullshit is this about letting your life just randomly unfold on its own terms? You know, making the steps by walking. In our time it may feel odd to us, but it comes from a notion of calling handed down from ancient insight into what it means to be human. It lies deep within the heart of every religious faith that I know of, but it's known by different names. Allowing what will be to be has been called providence or predestination, The Way or Wu Wei. The secularists call it flow. The Muslims, surrender. Que sera, sera! Your spiritual tap on the shoulder might show up as an intense dream that wakes you up in the middle of the night specifically calling your name to reorient you to the life you were meant to have, rather than the life you planned. Or that sense of knowing may manifest as extraordinary satisfaction in the life that you are already living. What will be, will be.

Responding fully to spiritual awakening means that you have—congratulations—discovered the awful truth that you are not as in charge of your own life as you were taught to believe. Yes, you may be making choices that will impact your life every single day. Big whoop. You get to have a little slice of free will. But so, so much has already been chosen for you. You didn't get to pick the genetic code of your body, like it or not. Nor did you fully determine the characteristics of your personality. You didn't decide which family you would be born into, and those fools who were your parents had quite a lot of power and influence on your life before you became capable of living on your own (and sometimes after). Even the native language that you speak and the socioeconomic life you find familiar are much more than likely products of how and where you arrived on this planet and took your very first breath.

Your soul knows something of who you are and who you are meant to be but may or may not be sharing that information. You didn't choose it. You *fell* into *this* life, not any other. It is a gift you have been given. Religion, or sometimes life itself, will find a way to remind you that your life is a gift that only uniquely you are capable of living. You got invited to this party called life. And we all know about celebrations and the gifts that come with them. Some fit us perfectly and some seem like a god-awful (pun intended) mistake.

Sure, check it out for yourself. You *can* actively try to be someone you are not, perhaps even with some success. But ultimately you are the one who will know if your life is being lived authentically—or if your life is being jammed into a box that doesn't fit. When you accept that you are being sent on this spiritual journey and begin to have some clue as to how to answer the big questions—"Who am I?" "Why am I here?" "What did I say 'yes' to?" and "What difference will I make?"—then it might be a good idea to let the real answers to those questions guide who you are becoming.

Whole industries out there would love to sell you the ultimate plan for achieving well-being and unlocking success. "Find your true purpose," they will say. They may even package their products as a means for those seeking an awakening to achieve it.

Don't be fooled by the allure of the perfect life. Those chasing happiness rarely catch it and ultimately will spend extraordinary amounts of time and money trying. And those who are encouraged to believe that an awakening will lead to prosperity and a guarantee of God's favor are likely to be gravely disappointed. The chase for meaning, though, sells—handsomely. But a snake oil promise is still only beneficial for the slippery souls who make a profit selling it.

Pursuing your calling, your authentic life experience, will likely frighten you and drain you, and quite possibly make you a crankier, more disagreeable person. You might become an unsuccessful, broke-ass nonconformist. You might be sent to do something hard or tedious or uncomfortable. Congratulations because you are going to love it. It means you will be authentically you with none of the pretending or posturing.

Kerra, you might think, *I'm reading this book so I could unlock and achieve maximum optimization of my spiritual life goals. You might tell me that awakenings suck, or that life is a mess, sure. But then you will tell me that it's all worth it, right?*

I also grew up thinking I could find clear meaning and a preferably well-paid purpose to life. I thought I could be good enough, smart enough, talented enough, and educated enough and that the whole world of opportunities would open up before me. That's not how my life has unfolded, and probably not yours either. I haven't always landed the job or loved everything about the job I got. My relationships have been messily human and full of both joys and heartbreak. I have tried very hard at times to be things I'm not. I still have plenty of work to do with my therapist and my spiritual director just to keep countering my own dumb expectations. But what I have realized over time is that all I needed was to be "enough" of me. No qualifiers necessary.

It's a good question, though, to wonder why there is so much fear and vulnerability in simply being yourself. Why is there overwhelming disappointment and the unpleasant discovery of my own wickedness that comes with exposure to the spiritual life? Why can't I be all that and a bag of chips? Aren't awakened people ever successful too? I mean, by the world's standards?

We want to know if it's worth it to follow the spiritual pathway. I can't tell you if it's going to feel worth it, because I'm not you. I don't know what life circumstances are like for you. I don't know if the pressure to succeed, or be happy, or please someone else's image of who you should be will derail your progress toward following your inner voice. I don't know if you will give yourself permission to even pause long enough to see if you can hear it. What I do know, from my own messy existence, is that the more I lean into following the nudges of the Spirit, the more I feel satisfied in my soul, and the more authentically "me" I become. Trying to predict where that will take me doesn't work. Wishing I could change the past to make my life simpler or happier doesn't work. Living in the present as fully as I can is the sweet spot, and I can only be good at that some portion of the time. However, living an authentic life matters. It matters because you get this one, right now, and no other. Might as well make it count.

Authenticity

Those of you who have felt an awakening experience or who have cultivated a long-standing spiritual practice may come to the uneasy conclusion you are being tapped by the Divine for a specific purpose. Gaining a new understanding of yourself as purposefully entwined with God's purpose for the world may come as a shock or a welcome change, but whatever you are coming to know seems so compelling that it cannot be ignored. And no matter what you do, the feeling of this purpose being specifically yours to follow will not go away. You may have been excited at first to be sent on a quest of personal discovery. But how do you get from "God called me out" to "Now I have to live this way"? That's the question: how can I live the life that Joseph Campbell describes as "waiting for me"?

Waking up and then finding yourself guided on your path by God is neither guaranteed to be the best thing nor the worst thing that ever happened to you. It is ultimately about living the life most authentic to you, and perhaps also not feeling completely alone as you face all the personal ups and downs of your pilgrimage.

Unfortunately many religious institutions want to coopt the job of mapmaker, telling everyone what the one and only correct route looks like, rather than playing a supporting role for religious travelers, and learning how to be fellow learners and companions for the journey. Fundamentalist religion would rather teach that a sense of awakening to God's path for you can only happen by some version of following their rules, some version of how meticulously you can jump through their systemic hoops to be a good person—by their standards.

At its worst, if your awakening is to a religious vocational calling, that can become just another example of adopting the curated life rather than awakening to your own. For clergy who first feel God's nudge toward a specific purpose, it can come as a shock that the institution will control your employment, and it may even control things like where you live and what kind of family you have. Give the institution power over your spiritual life, and you'll still be pulled by all the "should" and "supposed to" rules following conformity, which makes for organizational ease if everyone can be held to the same process, rules, and expectations. But then it doesn't include an appreciation for the messiness and the broad spectrum of all life's peculiarities. Those who muster the courage to talk about their spiritual path suddenly veering and how it truly transformed them usually seem a little nutty, especially to the religious institutions they might hope will honor their work.

But saying yes to awakening's call is less about adopting a particular religious mindset and more about accepting the life that has been given to you—the one that is exactly meant for you. Live it. Be it. Even if someone wants to make you feel less than or inadequate for not measuring up to the status quo, who cares? You shouldn't. It's your life, not theirs. Be who you are. Accept that you are exactly as you are meant to be, exactly as the Creator of the universe intends for you to be.

Living into your path takes courage, mostly the courage to act and feel different. And although this difference is actually a common thread in the religious mythology that Campbell loved so much, we tend to attribute superlative qualities to those few who actually seem able to do it. We hold them up as anointed, enlightened, chosen, or prophetic—when perhaps they weren't looking for reverence but were simply being themselves. And if anything, in telling their stories, they were encouraging those who would follow them to take their own spiritual paths.

Yes, there's some moral common ground among those we hold up as spiritual giants, but determining the difference between a religion and a cult often comes down to how vigilantly the leader demands to be obeyed at all times and at all costs. Jesus, Buddha, Muhammad, Moses, and a host of others did lead people into what they believed to be authentic spiritual paths, but the original material is typically far less structural, hierarchical, and rule-based than the systems some adherents have later created. In assessing your own calling, or if you're invited to walk with someone in discernment of their ability to be true to their calling, see if you sense in yourself or in them whether who you or they say they are matches who the person actually is. The more that's true, the more you and they will be revealed as examples of authentic spirituality.

Waking Up Every Day

What I mean by "answering the call" is not only the experience of a sense of awakening as described in previous chapters, but as intentionally and as fully as possible continuing to wake up every day living the path that awakening leads you on. You have found the path, discovered your direction, known God's presence, and you are there for it! You are answering your sense of purpose with the way you will live your life. *That* is answering the call, that is your calling. Author Gregg Levoy describes a calling as "a need for change" that is related to "an awakening of some kind." He adds, "A call is only a monologue. A return call, a response, creates a dialogue." Like Levoy, I believe that true awakenings ultimately require both change and a response on our part.

Levoy investigated many varied stories of people's callings for his book *Callings: Finding and Following an Authentic Life*. He reported that true awakenings guide people toward authenticity and integrity. Therefore, it is important to also know what a calling is not. For instance, some experiences seem like awakenings but aren't, and some people describe callings in ways not consistent with or conducive to life on the spiritual journey. There are so many misreads on what it means to live into one's own authentic life that I propose we look at three significant "not this" aspects that can merit our consideration and sharpen our understanding for the authentic.

Being Called Is Not Fatalism

Yes, you have a background. Yes, you are called to "fall into" your life, not plan it, but you *are not* doomed with or by your destiny. When the stories of the biblical prophets are told, as they are being called to speak God's truth, most of the time they are looking over their shoulder, wondering, *Was God really talking to me just now?*

Frequently, those being asked not only to live authentically but to question the level of truth-telling present in their own time and place, well, they don't really want the job. It's not sexy. It doesn't pay much. And people won't like you for doing it. I understand why life according to the world's script is more appealing. Those shoulds and supposed-tos are like the bumper rails in bowling. They keep you in the game and scoring points. You can feel good about yourself for having the willpower to operate correctly and in bounds.

The maddest people have gotten at me for something I've said in a sermon is when I've been rather "meh" about the concept of free will. Christianity especially has been played up as the religion that you choose for yourself and that you might not get into if your "yes" isn't enthusiastic enough. But once you become familiar with just how little control you have, you may even call into question if you are able to choose your own religion—or if it chose you.

But affirming the yes that's already inside of you—the you that is wholly you—isn't simply accepting your fate as some pawn in God's chess match. It's allowing the presence of the Divine to work in you, through you, in the ways that only your yes can make happen. God will always allow you to say no, or not now, or even eff off. In fact, you might benefit from being the one who pushes back a bit on God's choice. Sometimes a path begins with no. I never wanted to be a pastor. I hated spiritual direction the first time I tried it. I still cuss and drink and am not the finest example of human compassion there ever was. But I have found joy in walking the walk that seems to be the pathway that fits. And it also means that I'm not a smarmy preacher type who is in it for the sense of control of others. I can barely manage my own spiritual life, so any advice I usually give to others sounds far more like, "Learn from my mistakes," rather than, "Obey my rules so you'll succeed."

Your called life is solely *your* authentic life as it unfolds. You might as well play what you've been dealt rather than try to fool around and be something you're not. It sounds like fatalism, but really it is acceptance of your own gifts and your own limitations, acceptance of a purpose and a plan greater than you. And that acceptance is something humbling and empowering. It doesn't make you better than anyone else, and it doesn't make anyone else better than you.

Being Called Is Not Exceptional

You are awakened to a path, a direction, a calling. Awesome. But I don't think I will crush your spirits by saying you didn't earn it by being good. And you didn't pray it into being with your faithfulness. That's the beauty of digging into the artifacts of religious storytelling. If anything, God seems to choose the most unlikely individuals, people, and places to hold up as holy. Almost seems as though God is telling us, "Don't start thinking of yourself as special, rather think of yourself as someone who is saying yes, who isn't shutting down something that seems to be opening up."

Some spin an alternative to Joseph Campbell's observation toward living the life you've been given, and in the positive-thinking circles it's been dubbed "The Secret." It's the belief that what you wish for will come true—and it plays into the kind of fantasy life many of us have. If only I dream it, I can become it. It's a trick of the false prophets, terrible rulers, and smarmy preachers who have claimed to be specifically "God-chosen" so that they can be conferred with popularity, power, or wealth. It's those preachers who need jet planes and the freshest kicks. It's equating being called with being monetarily and popularly #blessed.

Yes, God calls people out of slavery and traumatic circumstances, and from a place of survival to an opportunity to thrive. But God is not known to call the rich to their riches or the powerful to their power in ways that suggest their stations are better than the rest of us. In his most famous set of teachings, Jesus said, "Blessed are the poor." His mom taught him that, and she was one of the lowly types—and a call answerer—who solidly affirmed the yes within her. Her acceptance speech to awakening began with, "My soul magnifies the Lord." Yes, that's what she said. How humble, how authentic, how powerful is that!

Being Called Is Not What You Get Paid For
(Though It Could Be)

In my line(s) of work, I've become friends with clergy colleagues. We bitch and moan about work just as much as any other profession, and mostly it is what you think it is. We complain about the people. It may be a wonderful vocation at times, but frankly, on many days, it's just a job. It's a job that isn't on the upper end of the pay scale either—like teachers and hospital staff, or anyone in a service industry of any kind.

You kind of have to love the work and believe you are there for a reason. It's not easy and it's not well-compensated. On most days, to be a spiritual leader, you have to like people at least as much as you like God. And often, I'm not sure which is harder.

The institutional denominational structures—particularly in Christianity-land—have taught clergy to believe that becoming a religious leader means achieving educational goals and passing ecclesiastical tests. There are hoops to jump through to become an ordained pastor in every branch of Christian tradition. They may not look exactly alike, but they're there. Other religious institutions impose similar "testing" for those who wish to lead, but I know less about what it takes to become a rabbi, imam, shaman, or guru.

Becoming part of the priestly crowd has been both my path and my calling, the voice I heard to leave the rut I was in and go, and the daily effort I put into waking up to the spiritual truth, again, even on those days when I don't want to. What I had to unlearn, though, was that a calling is not synonymous with a religious profession, or any job really. My call is not my job—though some traditions or people conflate the two with a ridiculous amount of overlap. I was awakened, over time, to understanding myself as a spiritual leader—which sometimes has played nice with my job and other times has been what has made keeping my job hell. Know that awakening to yourself may set you on the path to advocating for marginalized communities, fighting for justice, feeding the homeless, saving the earth, finding homes for stray dogs and cats, cleaning our waterways, or doing a vast number of things, whatever comes from your yes that is authentic to you. You may get paid for that work. You may not. Your nine-to-five job could be what you love that makes you the most authentic you possible. If so, that's amazing. Be thankful for that. Or it could be what puts food on the table so that your time can be spent serving on a board of a nonprofit, or making music or art.

Digging even a little bit deeper into our assumed truths, living in a capitalist economy dictates the belief that what we get paid for will be the thing that determines our worth. Nope. Not true. At least it's not the full truth. The full truth is found in awakening to living out the integrity of our whole lives. Therefore, it is important to say that I also intentionally made room for children in my life, even as I had no idea who they were going to be when they came into this world. My yes to being their mother is an unpaid and often thankless position, but I truly believe that my two kids were sent to me and my spouse so that we would learn from them. Despite what parenting books say, our children are not blank slates for us to mold to our liking. They are unique individuals with authentic lives of their own. My hardest job as a mother sometimes is to get out of their way.

And there are a multitude of other ways we are called to live fulfilling lives without making our pleasures into a side hustle. Being a creator does not mean you have to sell what you create. Make music. Make art. Write poetry. And for the love of God, do it badly. Do it because your heart says so. Being an influencer doesn't mean you have to go on TikTok. Influence your friends and family through meaningful conversation. Influence your environment by serving soul-satisfying food and decorating your living space for the hospitality of welcoming others into your home.

Our Response to Awakening: The Answered Call

Living into an awakened life, a spiritually transformed way of being, takes us back to the first questions we ask when beginning a quest. *Who am I? Why am I here? What have I said yes to? Who has sent me? What difference will my life make?* Becoming fully responsive to the call is then waking up every single day ready to find fresh answers that will deepen your yes to those questions. It's supposing that you will be here now for the life that you have, rather than always wishing that it turned out another way.

In the spiritual guidance program where I took classes to be a spiritual director, Ben Campbell, the program's founder, taught that an authentic calling would have two parts to it—location and vocation. Location can be where you are quite literally: where do you live, who surrounds you in your circle of influence, and why are you being asked to make a difference in that particular place? And it is also the nature of your identity, questions young people today ask with the same fervor they've always asked, and their elders have often dismissed as frivolous. But location is about the identities that shape who we are—race, gender, sexuality, social circumstance, ideals, perceptions, personality, and beliefs. They are where you find yourself, and that matters. Identifying who you are is the first step in accepting your authentic self and your path.

The second part is vocation. What are you going to do with that? How will you, the you who is uniquely you, engage the world around you? Whether you choose it for yourself or it seems to be chosen for you by your circumstances and constraints, each person is living out their own vocation in the world, be it through a job, a role, or simply by living the authentic day-to-day life.

In examining the spiritual life, we often try to complicate what is simple. Who you are and what you do merit your awareness and your attention. It's worth contemplating how we got here, and what we intend to do with our "one wild and precious life." Thank you, poet and mentor to many, Mary Oliver, for the question that matches or perhaps surpasses Joseph Campbell's insight on calling as the life that is waiting for us.

To explore what it means to respond to your own awakening by following the paths (all of them that speak to you) and therefore answer your (whole life) calling, you will have to put in the work of reflection and self-discovery. It's easy to simply fall into the trap of a meaningless daily grind. Truth be told, most days are made up of mundane tasks and I don't feel like I'm living my yes-to-awakening when I'm folding laundry or answering emails. But overall, perhaps I am. I am living in a time when the washer and dryer do the bulk of the work for me. I am living in an era when a letter that I write can pop into that recipient's inbox almost as immediately as when I hit Send.

But because I desire to live into a bigger understanding of who I am and who I am meant to be in this world, from time to time I pause and reflect on all those things that curiously make me, me. And the awakening moments that happen when I become curious, or explore or reject my faith, or when I'm joyful or suffering, or trying to let go of previous assumptions—all that makes up the considerations for what my spiritual life, my awakened-to and authentic life, will be.

Most sacred writings, including the Bible, tell stories of exactly that: the reflections of people in their own times and places trying to understand who they are and who they are meant to be. Some of the stories, like the books of Jonah, Esther, and Job, really lay it on thick, with the exaggerated states of being in which the characters find themselves. But sometimes that exaggeration, with its bolder lines, helps us to find parallel truths to our own lives.

Jonah's first response to awakening was a definite no. He boarded a ship instead of going to Nineveh to preach repentance. Who can blame him? Esther, because of her context, her beauty, and proximity to the king, as well as her culture and heritage, was able to call off the obliteration of her people. Job lost everything he thought was important in his life, seeking answers among his friends, who ended up being no help at all. Only when he encountered God and heard God speak did he awaken to something shifting in him.

The awakening, the insight, the nudge to change or do something different might not turn out in any way that you expect. But to pay attention to the nudge is to be willing to be surprised.

For some time, I thought I was being nudged to look for a new pastorate, maybe a higher-up role in the institutional church. God can be such a tease sometimes. I got several "almost" interviews that hammered away at my self-confidence when it turned out that I was "second-best." But in that time of nudging toward ... something, I had a dream. In it I received a full-on book idea and the basic outline for this book. Silly me, I thought the book was the side quest, the maybe hustle, and that the real opportunity, meaning the full-time paying opportunity, would be just around the next corner. Nevertheless, even when search committees kept saying no, doors kept opening for me to talk about and write about spiritual awakening. A light kept shining in one direction, and I said yes. I wrote down the book from the dream. The outline kept growing. I started imagining how the chapters fit together. That kept me going, and kept me writing, pondering if my spiritual roles were not all connected to a congregation or the church. When we are trying to interpret our own sense of answering the awakenings in us, looking backward can be more informative than speculating about the future. Behind me I see a path that clearly led me, while ahead I see only mist and generalities.

Sometimes we pursue a direction because we think it's a divine nudge, but maybe it's the start of a winding

172 | True Awakening

path toward something utterly different than we initially expected. If you are a *Bluey* cartoon watcher, you might recall the story "The Farmer" in an episode called "The Sign." Bluey's family is thinking about a move, something we tend to associate with pursuit of goals or direction. And it shows the characters going through all their own emotions about how they are reacting as kids, and how the parents are expressing their own uncertainty. Then the schoolteacher reads an illustrated book with the parable of the farmer. In the parable, the farmer has things that either look like good luck or bad luck from the point of view of the observer. When the farmer is told, "Wow, that was really good luck," he says, "We'll see," and the same is true when they tell him that it must have been bad luck. Again the farmer says, "We'll see." Patience and waiting allow the farmer to see the much bigger picture, like when his son breaks his leg riding a horse, it looks like bad luck, but when they come to conscript for the army and he can't go, maybe it's good luck. Sometimes, our bad luck, our nos, and our rejections tell us even more than what seems to go so well for us.

Awakenings to new directions and paths are as unique as the individuals who experience them, and judging someone else's experiences from the outside is problematic. What we know from the inside is, it's about making a difference, that pesky question from the quest chapter. You might feel well placed to be a casino owner, but then the question becomes a nudge: Are you contributing positively to your community with your endeavor? Does the good that you might be able to give (jobs, a fun time for winners) outweigh the problems (gambling addictions, taking money from the poor looking for a break)? Does the income allow you to take care of an incapacitated family member? A job can be a job. Even a family caretaking role can feel much more like an obligation than a nudge to give of yourself. Again, self-reflection is key.

Some of us are stubborn—like I am, like Jonah was— and it will take multiple attempts from the Divine to get our attention. Sometimes the calling will bloom like a flower and just feel exactly right. Sometimes your yes will be to a job that you love; sometimes your job will be the side hustle that allows you to write the story of your dreams. Sometimes it won't be related to what you get paid for at all.

Being awakened and answering with your yes is about trust. You are trusting your own inclinations and experiences to guide you to your life's meaning and purpose. You trust a divine plan and a purpose for each and every individual human being on this planet. What if—amazing thought—our lives are providentially meant to go exactly as they go? Does that enthrall you or depress you?

Once you have given your yes in response to that nudge, the awakening; once you have wrestled with what the path is, and how you get to walking it; then it's onward to living into your authentic life. You'll live your true yes to the divine call to turn in a direction, with all the highs and lows of it, with all the mess that makes you question and question again how to be most fully you, so you will be most fully what the world needs you to be. And then your regular life will be connected to the larger picture as you stay your own weird self, aware that the boring parts, the laundry and the dishes, are also all right. Not every moment needs to be interpreted as signs and wonders for it to be full of meaning and purpose.

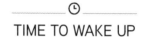

TIME TO WAKE UP

If the awakening is the nudge to change,
And the journey is the path toward the change,
Looking back, how have you changed?
Looking forward, how are you being changed?
Wake up—every day—and every day will be a new beginning.
What is it, as Mary Oliver asks, that you will do with your one wild and precious life?

9

EMBRACE THE STRANGE AND BRACE FOR BORING
Meeting the Wonders and Living the Mundane

The soul is like a wild animal—tough, resilient, savvy, self-sufficient and yet exceedingly shy. If we want to see a wild animal, the last thing we should do is go crashing through the woods, shouting for the creature to come out. But if we are willing to walk quietly into the woods and sit silently for an hour or two at the base of a tree, the creature we are waiting for may well emerge, and out of the corner of an eye we will catch a glimpse of the precious wildness we seek.

—Parker Palmer

THE WILD AND TENDER PARTS of our human experience are so difficult to describe. Though they resist easy categories or labels, others may be quick to dismiss the awe of your spiritual encounters as either lacking evidence or not fitting a particular mold. Talking about any connection of your spirit with a more universal Spirit requires either prophetic boldness or deep trust in your experience as well as gauging how your words might be received—hopefully, with openness and nonjudgment.

Start a story with, "I think I heard God talking to me," and you can imagine how others will call you crazy. Worse is, given their response, you may begin to doubt your own experience or simply stop talking about it. Even if your moment of Zen felt like one of the most real encounters of your life, you yourself are likely already questioning if that voice, or vision, or symbolic impression could possibly mean—anything.

Even those we think of as confirmed spiritual giants, who had religions founded in their names, have had detractors question their sanity. Then again, so did all the self-proclaimed religious leaders who had their followers drink the Kool-Aid or watch for Halley's Comet to come take them off this planet. So when it gets strange, and your experience is out of the realm of what we generally consider to be regular human interactions, how will you know if you had a spiritual encounter or just a break with reality?

Among the questions you might ask are,

Was my spiritual experience real?
Was my spiritual experience similar to those others have experienced?
Was my spiritual encounter unique and meant especially for me?
How do I tell what I should trust from what I shouldn't trust—spiritually?

This is a dangerous area to play in. Who am I to discern if you've really communicated with God or if there's a tumor pressing on your brain? (Both—or neither—could be true at the same time.) Fortunately, you're not alone. Many who have come before us have sought to answer those questions. And—good news or bad news, however you see it—ultimately you yourself must decide if your experiences are generally aligned with recognized spiritual experiences. Often these begin with a validation that, yes, there is a spiritual component to the life in which we all participate. And, no, you don't have to prove the existence of God to know that you have been graced by a brush with a spiritual connection. And your experience doesn't even have to match up with the expectations of your religious community. God will speak to you in *your* language. Otherwise, how would you hear what you were meant to hear? And if comes in the form of hearing, "You are fucking beautiful," in your heart and mind to know those words to you are God's presence, that's quite all right. And don't presume you misheard God, autocorrecting the message to "ducking." Let the message to you be what it is.

When someone wants to tell me a strange story about how they heard a message from God—in a voice, in a dream, in a serendipitous circumstance—I am all ears. I love those stories, and they are very much a part of the human experience. It is a joy and delight to discover that others have truly felt the awe and wonder of knowing closeness with the Divine.

When and where do such moments take place? Good question. Are they ordinary or extraordinary? Yes—both. Spiritual experiences ultimately reveal how paradoxical life is, valuing both the particular and the whole. Can you invoke it or buy one or somehow choose your own spiritual adventure?

Tough question. As mentioned earlier, whole industries have developed around providing you with a spiritual experience. You could travel to the "thin places"—deemed to be so beautiful and extraordinary that the divine presence must be felt there. Some people go to religious conferences or silent retreats hoping to get away from their ordinary lives enough to have that mountaintop experience. But you can't force it. Not in Sedona. Not at an ashram. Not for a thousand dollars and the promise of a personalized realization plan.

You might sign up for a breathwork session or decide to go to church on a random Sunday morning. Perhaps

Embrace the Strange and Brace for Boring | 179

one of these opportunities will be exactly what you need, but then again, once you get there, it might feel smarmy or insignificant. You may eat, pray, love yourself to a holy encounter, or just have a nice vacation. Should you go out in search of enlightenment, you may find it elusive. But if you take time to look up in the trees in your own backyard, maybe then you will have a moment of clarity in your otherwise not-so-eventful spiritual life.

Basically, spiritual moments aren't a commodity. You can't put a guarantee on an outcome. Go ahead and take that retreat. Try that practice. But if it isn't a fit, it may just not be the right time or the right adventure. Putting yourself in the emotional and physical space to allow God to reach you is more fruitful than pursuing the elusive moment of rapture and delight. And I hate that shit: openness and allowing as a spiritual practice. Ugh. We want enlightenment on our own time schedules and in that moment when we need picking up off the basement floor—and yet that dark night may be what clicks as your God-moment more than the three-day vegan yoga retreat and sound bath in the Colorado mountains that will set you back two grand.

Can you begin to sense those wild and tender moments right in front of you? For some, it takes that hard break from the ordinary to allow your eyes to see. But it's not unavailable to the ordinary person. What's more, people on the margins may somehow see with a spiritual clarity that makes those who have privilege uncomfortable. Why do *they* have such assurance in the knowledge of God and access to feeling blessed when the middle-class suburbanite gives up on having a meaningful existence when their yoga class can't deliver both sacred truth and a slimmer waistline?

These are the reversals so common in an examination of the spiritual life. Those who are "good at it" come away saying that it's as close to you as your breath, and neither a passport nor a week of silence in a monastery is necessary to achieve connection. It's not the rich and powerful who show up in Jesus's Sermon on the Mount. Rather, those who are blessed are the invisible masses who might know God best: the poor, the meek, the humble, the troubled. Jesus—well, he nailed it. Gratitude for life can come from anywhere—*anywhere*. And such gratitude leaves us feeling blessed, knowing that for the present moment, we truly have enough.

And just like those gratitude-in-knowing moments, I believe there still *are* ways to prepare oneself for receiving a spiritual awakening, but it's pretty standard religious stuff, and kind of boring. Those who go out to seek the spiritual often want the big aha moment, but attention to a spiritual life is more often about regular meditation, ritual, holding silence in nature, and being patient in observing ordinary life. Want a brush with the Divine? Chop wood, carry water. Also practice more kindness, more quiet, and adopt the possibility that you can live with less control over how your life turns out. Allowing again, right?

Embrace the Strange and Brace for Boring | 181

This is no guarantee either. Some will try the bullet train to spiritual enlightenment with a psychedelic-induced opening or a midlife crash or any life-altering event—good or bad. Such events may begin the process of exploring the spiritual side of life. That's the problem with the unexplainable—there are no exact words to cover it. Be it a vision, a voice, or an awe-inspiring moment of ecstasy spent in joy or terror, something happens to you or through you and being able to make sense of it requires that you suspend the limits and language of ordinary experience, because you caught a glimpse of the spiritual world beyond it or within it.

These events or openings are what we usually call "spiritual awakenings"—the *moment* when that story seems to pull at us in real time and call us toward a much larger perspective. The voice spoke truth. The vision was astonishingly real. The joy overwhelming. The terror more than I could bear but I lived to tell about it. It's the scales falling from our eyes.

I get it. We like transformation stories that rely on a climactic moment to mimic the resolution we can get from our favorite novel. But the awakening itself is everything. All. Of. It. For me, it was a moving kaleidoscope: from the fascination of watching animals from a treehouse, to my sitting in church next to the pastor's kind wife who took me under her wing in a grandmotherly way, to a nudging for me to pay attention to my ongoing interest in religious studies.

Yeah, I got an amazing lifetime opportunity to trip on a couch at Johns Hopkins, but it is the whole integration process that matters. True awakening is best described as a lifetime of attesting to the journey, not a one-off event. Take the apostle Paul's backstory, for example: when he was still known as Saul, he traveled on the Damascus road, met a blinding light, fell to the ground, and experienced something like scales falling from his eyes. But then he changed his name to Paul and got to work—both to the hard inner work of changing his zealous and destructive attitude toward Jesus's followers, and to the outer work of reaching others with the awakening that changed his life.

The event that rocked your world may or may not be as vividly remembered a few years from now, but over time you will learn how it impacted you, changed you, and transformed your life as you are now living it.

There's assessing for authenticity and then there's working on the narrative of your spiritual life—that's where these spectacular spiritual occasions are truly transforming and influential, not only in the life of the person who experienced a "moment," but in the lives of the community affected by that person and in the work done inspired by a holy encounter.

I read, watched, listened, and learned with great interest as the folks at Johns Hopkins devised their own methods for assessing my levels of mystical encounter within their study of religious professionals tripping on psilocybin. Yes, they asked me a whole lot of questions about my experience—those who were in the room with me and those who were taking notes afterward. But they also assessed me through the perspective of three others, people I was in close contact with, whom I chose as "reporters" who were later asked about any changes in my behavior or attitudes. Those hosting the study were looking for signs my life had really changed, looking for anything that was measurably different in my life after that intense encounter, anything that might indicate spiritual seeing.

As I went through the aspects of the study, I appreciated the model. Spiritual transformation might be experienced in our own minds and hearts, but it doesn't mean much if it lets me be the very same kind of asshole I've always been in the world. Awakening is about change. That's what makes it uncomfortable, and then ... strangely interesting, and then perhaps monotonous as we seek to repeat the practices that reconnect us to who we are beginning to believe we can be in this world.

Authentic versus Narcissistic

There really are some ways of assessing the occasional powerful spiritual experience to understand if it tips the scale toward awakening with authentic growth or if it simply adds to a collection of events led by narcissistic self-importance.

Maybe someone says to you, "God spoke to me."

Awesome, I think. And then I consider what other information might be revealing.

Do they think God only speaks to them?

If so, that's not cool. It's an aberration of the mystical, thinking you are uber special and that you have been tapped to be the mediator of God's plan for others. Religious leaders fall into this trap quite easily, starting to feel favored and prioritized among God's people.

Do they say, "God told me to tell you . . ."?

Also not cool. It's an aberration of the prophetic. The prophets always seem to include themselves as recipients of the prophetic message. They talk about God being mad at *us*, not mad at *those individuals over there*. Judgment is not a pronouncement that solely tells us what we want to hear about what's wrong with other people. When the prophets talk about what God wants from us, you can bet it's going to include compassion, justice, and the very hard work of loving people who might not be just like us.

Do they go on being a great big jerk?

More uncoolness. If God is truly speaking to them, there's probably a benevolent outcome somewhere around the corner. If not, it's fair to wonder if it was really God they were experiencing, or the desire to be more God-like. You might know a politician, or a billionaire, or a religious television personality seemingly chummy with

God who claims to have personal knowledge of God's plans. Such claims should make you question God's ability to break through to humanity when the voice or vision comes with that baggage of exclusivity.

However, if someone is humbled by what they heard God saying, or challenged to try another path, or beams with the energy of divine love, well, you probably are talking with a person who has encountered something far larger than themselves. The strange thing they heard or saw or felt is real. It has the power to be transformative. As you hear their story, it may seem like a lot of gray areas to wade through, but this is just part of the mess of spiritual transformation. It takes thoughtfulness and examination to figure out what really might be going on. When someone tells you they have had an encounter with the holy one, neither take it nor dismiss it outright. It will bear out. And that will be true of your own experiences as well. Did you claim to hear what you wanted to hear in prayer, or is God awakening you to take a deeper look at yourself?

Consolations and Desolations

Spiritual awakening moments and the transformations that follow them are going to come through what we experience as both highs and lows. In the world of spiritual formation, sometimes these are considered *consolations* and *desolations*. Does God seem to be consoling you, comforting you with little signs and affirmations—your favorite song on the radio at just the right time, the teacher who appears to offer you advice just when you need it most? These are blessings—moments of grace or joy or peace, an invitation to trust that you are on the right path. Desolations, as you might have guessed, are different. The rough message. God wakes you up in the night and you gasp: suddenly you know what you don't want to be doing anymore. Sometimes the desolation is the sense of nothingness. No sense of God, or that there is no God. You are alone, and yet you experience a longing for the companionship of something completely other. That longing can bring us toward God, just as the thank-yous of gratitude can as well. What a mess, right? It's all the messenger.

Invitations to wake up to the spiritual life are all over the place. And where does it leave you? Feeling vulnerable, probably. Ah, vulnerability, where we allow ourselves to feel our feelings. Vulnerability—when the anger, sadness, joy, or love feel so incredibly close that the whole world seems to be joining us in this dance, whatever steps it is here to teach us. The invitations to vulnerability teach me that God is our partner in that dance, and God is leading. I'm a follower. Spiritual acumen comes from being aware of the present moment and being able to allow life, as it is, to show you the way.

This openness, the willingness to be the dance partner who is led, this awareness of consolations and desolations come as we are actively attuned to right now. What is it that puts you in this moment, in this place, in this situation right now? You can noodle around with that question in a journal. Or meditate, practice gratitude, swear, and curse—whatever you need to do. But whether you decide to examine the highs and lows of the past ten minutes or choose to do an evening review at the end of the day, you'll find those times of blessing and those times of longing offering their wisdom and their wonder to you as treasured gifts. Such spiritual encounters may bring you close to the Divine or may throw you into challenge mode. Let them. God is speaking to us, helping us cast our visions, meeting us where we dream our dreams.

Believing in God—or Knowing God?

Again, the wild and tender parts of our human experience vary widely and thrive best within a nonjudgmental grounding that takes such diversity into account. That requires being kind with yourself as well as validating the experiences of others. The bifurcation of belief that has happened—particularly in Christianity, but perhaps in other religions as well—says that you believe or you don't. That swift judgment puts you either in or outside of the community, causing great pain. This litmus test of spiritual connection is reductive (putting it nicely) and shitty (to say how I really feel). You can probably hear those words of judgment:

Do you believe in God? Are you saved?

Proof questions don't give us a whole lot of information about how to really experience holiness. They are a doctrinal preservation of little-t truth, and don't acknowledge our spiritual moments of awe and wonder that give us a glimpse of the Big capital-T Truth. Doctrine rarely, if ever, communicates the heartbeat of the Divine to us.

How do you know God?

Now that's a much richer question. What such moments of awe and consolation, or terror and desolation, are meant to do is to help us really know God because God knows us. I care far less about whether spiritual leaders believe in any one tenet or expression of their faith. What I want to know is if they have felt God's presence or absence in their lives in a tangible way. An awakened person will have at least a few things to answer when it comes to that rich question. And the beauty of it is that these are not boxed answers. If you ask ten different people, you'll have ten different answers. It's not the consistency of doctrine, that's for damn sure. But it does allow you to understand that your own personal connection with God is exactly right for you because it was exactly given to you—the you that is authentically you. Then you have your whole entire life to ponder what that means and to live and direct your life in alignment with that knowledge.

The Ordinariness of It All

Well, shit. So all this magnificent and melancholy stuff gives us a way to talk about how we know holiness in our lives, and that holiness seems to last for about a half-second in the grand scheme of things. You can experience divine ecstasy in one moment and then turn around knowing that the laundry isn't going to do itself. I know I'll still irritate my husband, annoy my children, and have frustrations with my parents. Life goes back to being ordinary so damn fast.

That's where spiritual practices and the work of integration come in. I return to who I want to be on my prayer cushion or when I take a few precious minutes of reclining in savasana. I go to church, sometimes because it's my job, but other times because I need to hear ancient texts and pray some prayers with other people. I look into the eyes of my precious family and friends knowing that they come from pure divinity, but also see that there's so much more to them that till this moment I've absolutely taken for granted.

A spiritually transformed life will not be a perfect life. Highs. Lows. Messiness. And a whole lot of boredom stringing it together. That's the insight: Chop wood. Carry water. To do the ordinary with intent and connection to the moment happening right now, that's the way.

My theology mentor, Doug Ottati, was keen to introduce all his students to the obscure Puritan writer

Richard Baxter. Baxter wrote about how to have a "good" life in different professions, for he believed that you had to find your own ways of practicing exactly who God was calling you to be. A physician has to care about patients and understand that cost should not be prohibitive to getting care. I've often thought about the lessons of this principled way of being over the years. An ordinary life can become extraordinary just by living it with intent—awake and aware of how your own actions affect the lives of others. That's how you embrace the strange and brace for boring. First you receive the sparks, but then it's up to you to maintain the fire.

Ah, Yes, Spiritual Transformation

What kind of life will you have when you live your own truth? You've been through those nudges to change that have awakened you to new insights about yourself and your world—through the highs and lows of your own spiritual journey. You've responded to those insights with actions—answering the call through all the distractions that make it messy to hear distinctly what to do next. You yearn for that life of spiritual transformation—to live aware and attuned to the divine presence in your life. What does it look like to live that way?

I hear the answer to that question in the voice of the genie from Disney's *Aladdin*, who talks about the whole genie gig by saying, "Phenomenal cosmic power!

Itty-bitty living space!" Living the spiritually transformed life means that some days you will be awash with the extraordinary magnitude of all the spiritual, soulful energy in the universe, but then, practically in the same moment, you will realize the smallness of your circle of influence. The two are related.

In knowing the divine presence in the intimacy of co-creating your spiritual life with that presence, once you see the unitive oneness in the power and the intricate interconnectedness of all that is, you can't unsee it. The beauty, grace, and kindness that are available to you will now always be available to you. Again, as the spiritual giants say, access to holiness may seem like it is enshrined in the temples and glorified in cathedrals, or only found on the shores of Iona or in the desert of Sedona, but truly, it will be as close as your breath.

So, it all comes back to trusting God and letting go. That again. Even though I am but one person, bound by my own time and granted my own itty-bitty living space, the contributions of my life matter in the heart of God. That's a huge realization, transformational.

Oddly, my whole journey toward writing this book was a crazy exercise in getting to know that truth. I've shared a few nuggets of my story already, but it was truly a combination platter of embracing the strange (listening to a dream) and bracing for boring (as they say, writing a book is maybe 10 percent inspiration and 90 percent sitting down and getting words to appear on a screen).

When I look at how Teresa of Ávila or Julian of Norwich had their own moments of divine inspiration but then lived in a time when they had to pen their words out longhand, I am so, so grateful for modern technology and the computer age.

Details of my story and how this book got into your hands will reveal just how the spiritually transformed life is not exactly glamorous or serene. It's still all the mess of real life—perhaps amplified.

In the wee hours of February 19, 2023, a kind of completion of a vision came to me, tying threads together. At that point in my life, I was feeling intense restlessness and anticipating the need for a significant life change. (Awakening!) I was interviewing for a ladder-climbing kind of job, thinking that might be what God was wanting me to pursue because I am due for the kind of salary and benefits a job like that could provide, right? After all, I am a fabulous preacher and a deserving pastor. Though I loved the church I was serving at the time, I had been yearning for something different, something that seemed to be "more." More challenging. More diverse and interesting. And frankly, more successful in the world's eyes.

I had already encountered quite a few nos prior to that night, some from my own "not the right fit" category, some from lengthy interview opportunities that ended up with nada. (Lows!) I looked for work some distance away, and some of the jobs included travel requirements. My spouse, also in restless mode, had already taken a job with an eight-month contract ninety minutes from our home, and we weren't sure if it would become a more permanent position or end with completion of his transitional role. In this iteration of our nomadic job review, I didn't know yet if my vocational trajectory would be leading or trailing. I worried if our kids would find excitement or dread in any changes we might make. Everything was uncertain and felt shaky at best.

For my own sanity in such a chaotic time, I decided to take a course through the Center for Action and Contemplation on the mystic Teresa of Ávila. (Curiosity! Teachers!) The online talks by Mirabai Starr and James Finley were soothing to my soul, and reading *The Interior Castle* helped me discern that my job hunt wasn't even the most interesting part of the journey I was going through. Teresa was a solid companion, not only in what she was writing, but in how she was writing. She often broke the fourth wall, addressing her readers directly to complain about the task of writing. She felt unprepared for it, or at least hinted to her male superiors (another time and all) that she was not fit to write as a woman. I'm not sure if she was suffering from imposter syndrome, or merely being demure so that they might take her seriously. The way she talks about worldly distractions as a barrier to the enlightenment found in the most inner, most sacred parts of our lives, well, that felt painfully real. (Damn distractions!)

Then one night, that reality woke me up at what I've begun to think of as the God-hour, about 3 a.m. Clear as a bell, the message came: write about spiritual awakening not just by writing about the mystics like Teresa, but about what awakening looks likes now, in and for my own time.

Of course, I was now wide awake and couldn't just roll over and go back to sleep. So I got up out of bed, grabbed a stack of Post-it Notes and a pen and started sorting ideas and outlining a book as thoughts came at me way, way too fast. I put them all over an empty wall in our house, a collage of sticky notes. (Inspirational writing high!)

Sundays, I am used to speaking my words in a context that makes them sound like God's words, sometimes having had that sense of divine inspiration, sometimes not so much. This can be a bit terrifying in the moment, but I could always rest assured that by the end of that day, in the minds of others, what was going to stick would, and anything that was drivel would likely be forgotten. Two thousand words, max. That was my writing to that point. Sometimes I could choose whether to turn a sermon into a Facebook post with a tad more longevity, so that words would linger. Sermons are a craft that aren't as permanent as one might think.

Now, the inspiration to write a book felt different—exhilarating and intimidating. Of course fears came: What if I never finish it? What if it becomes too hard or takes too much time and consumes the rest of my

Embrace the Strange and Brace for Boring | 195

life's obligations? What if I get bored and just stare at a keyboard? What if I take the next church job and the writing stalls out? What if I don't take a church job and all this writing leads to nothing?

The 3 a.m. outline changed multiple times. Some things remained. I had to sit my ass down and work on chapters. (Boredom!) The nighttime inspiration didn't give me the whole book. It gave me a start. And it would have to come together with diligence and work. I would still be on the lookout for a paying main gig.

By the time of that February encounter, I had already given notice to the church I was serving, knowing that my life was going to change somehow, and that a move to another place was likely, whether it was following a job for me or for my husband. My congregation was gracious and kind, and we had an ending that felt "right." But then, over that summer, the bottom fell out of our family plans. There was no physical move. I didn't have another job to go to, and it turned out that my husband's position ended when his contract was complete. By the end of June, we were both jobless in a downturned economy. By any count, that's stressful. (Mess!)

And here I was writing a book about trusting God and letting go. (Also, irony!) There was absolutely nothing else for me to do except let go—or jump into a terrible panic. Only hindsight made it clear that we were listening, and my spouse and I were where we needed to be. We collected our rainy-day resources and shored up the confidence to continue doing the work we felt was ours to do. And I felt entrusted with the contents of the dream as a key to what would be next. As we waited for the opportunities to arise to make an income again, we also knew we were incredibly fortunate to be able to weather a financial drought and be okay. So many go through so much more, where a job loss means losing everything. Yet anytime a big blow-up happens and things go down, it can feel insurmountable. In my own storyline, the circumstances delivered a biblical kind of opportunity to go through yet another time of having to live my own truth: trust in the benevolence of the Spirit and the trajectory of the universe, and the belief that hope is not futile. It's meaningful and even practical in many ways.

So, as a family we made decisions and kept hoping and planning for our futures. I continued to write. Some days were wonderful. Other days were depressing and included endless doom scrolls of employment opportunities. We went from paying for our health insurance through the Affordable Care Act to being eligible for Medicaid. Answering the call to use my words felt both beautiful and painful, especially in the midst of one of the messiest, stressful, what-the-hell-will-be-next times in my life. (Desolation!)

Eventually, we both found work and remained in the place we reaffirmed as "home." The restlessness had shifted our focus. We were, without a doubt, doing things differently. We understood the importance of relying, not only on ourselves, but on our community—family, neighbors, friends, and connected relationships. What it takes to thrive cannot be denied. It takes a village! (Consolation!)

God knows all this. Human beings are meant to be in socialized relationships, and the strategies and struggles we encounter with our closest connections are a big, big piece of living the spiritual life. It's as important as any vocational journey. Your spouse, children, closest friends, business partners, coworkers, bosses, clients, or congregants, they are all present to help you reflect on your calling in life and the meaning you make from your circumstances. (Loving God, loving neighbors!)

It was through reconnecting with the intersection of the spirituality and psychedelics space that I met people who helped me in the writing process and trajectory of this book, as I began to understand this writing could be a gift offered for a broader community. It now felt like a culmination of all the things that have been on the path were forming out of the mist in front of me. It has been said, a million times, we make our path by walking it. We write our story by putting the words on a page. We find our spiritual life by living it. There's no grand secret. But there is amazement and joy. (Letting go of outcomes and letting life unfold!)

Ultimately, there is always something gained from listening to the Spirit's voice. It might feel like a nudge or a push, but when your spirit is aligned with the Spirit, life will feel authentic and hopeful. You will have an effect on your world, although maybe not "the" world. We sometimes get too bold in thinking we will change everything for everyone. It's sufficient to be a main character in your world, to offer your gifts to your circle, to allow your experience to be transformative.

Before the written word, before any codified doctrine about God, there were people experiencing the holy who chose to tell their stories. I began to see myself as within a tradition of those stories that are born from my experience in community, for the benefit of this community. Some of it may be helpful. All of it could be helpful. But if it's not, I still recognize that the divine presence is in all and through all. The scandal of the particular journey remains.

In my own particularity, I have sought to be a keen observer of my own life. I have been religious and antireligiosity. I have been a spiritual leader only because I know it's everything to be a spiritual follower. I have been transformed and I am walking into the mist of my next transformation.

TIME TO WAKE UP

Wake up! This is your life!

Where are your nudges to change? Greet your awakening with joy or dread, but welcome it fully.

Where are your highs and lows? Travel along the spiritual journey, taking along worthy companions.

Where are your consolations and desolations? Trust the Spirit's ability to reach you where you are.

Where is your mess? Open your eyes wide to the truth—as you sort out the through lines of your own story.

Where is your transformation? Maybe it's in the compilation of all those moments. Your one and only life (at least this go around), small as it may seem at times, is connected to the larger spiritual narrative. You are engaged with phenomenal cosmic power! Live life as though you know that in your bones. You are limited to the body you live in—itty-bitty living space. So wash dishes, chop wood, carry water. Use your inspiration to either get up and go or sit your butt down and do the hard work that you are meant to do. Engage the strange. Brace for boring. Your spiritual life awaits!

10

BEGIN AGAIN
Turning with the Cycle of Life

Let nothing disturb you. Let nothing upset you. Everything changes. God alone is unchanging. With patience all things are possible. Whoever has God lacks nothing. God alone is enough.

—Teresa of Ávila

All shall be well, and all shall be well, and all manner of things shall be well.

—Julian of Norwich

TRUE AWAKENINGS ALLOW US TO KNOW our inner selves. They also shape who we will be in the world. Transformational, right? But ultimately, how do we go about asking the big life questions that are an integral part of living on a fragile planet and working with the answers we receive? Are our interpretations with no reliable proof nothing other than our own assurances? Is what I experience of the spiritual life real? Did my experiences even happen as I remembered them? Are my interpretations of mystical events accurate? Is there meaning to be drawn from the pieces of spiritual input that I've strung together? Is my inner voice reliable? Are the insights I seem to have received from outside myself true? Is it really my divine source speaking to me or just the effects of spicy food rumbling my guts in the middle of the night? And those are just my personal questions.

Long ago John Calvin intuited that the only sound knowledge and wisdom that we possess is knowledge of God and of ourselves, and he thought those two things were intimately intertwined with each other. He believed that the more we explored that wisdom, the better we would understand the place of humanity in the world. At times, frankly, God-knowledge is too beyond, "too wonderful for me," as the psalmist laments. But the more curious I seem to be about myself, my friend, my neighbor, and all the interactions I have with my world, the more alive my spirit becomes.

I find this mysterious adventure of striving toward an understanding of divine truth and love of self and neighbor to be just about the most interesting thing I could do with my life. But at the same time, it takes a willingness to grow and change to welcome this capacious and ever-widening understanding of holiness, the kind that has the power to transform my life.

The spiritual life is going to be hard primarily because change is hard. We might know how to do it, but often don't because it costs too much. Look, there are plenty of meaningful pursuits for making a difference in this old world. The paths are many. The question remains: will we choose to follow the pursuits that appear before us in moments of spiritual clarity? We question whether we can go in this or that direction for a variety of reasons. We too often choose the path of "my own way," believing we already have all the answers we are ever going to need. Yeah, no. Awakening people are those who have said yes to being led. They are the ones who pack everything up and go when the spiritual guide in front of them says, "Follow me."

But even when in the full flow of following the divine source, we can get misdirected, make missteps. The path toward transformation reminds us, repeatedly, that even though we will have opportunities to benefit and grow from insights and awakenings, we will also experience the allure of vanity, the pain of regret, and the possibility of getting stuck on generational repeat until we are so over it that we are ready to try anything different. Transformation is both an uphill slog and a downhill slide. Just when you think you've reached a mountaintop, you'll crest a plateau and realize that you have a long way up yet to go. The humble may be exalted as Jesus taught—but only after they've been humbled about a bazillion times.

I don't know whether to count this as a blessing or a curse, but when you start allowing your awakening moments to change you and change how you express who you are, it will call into question the familiar family patterns you wanted to change but haven't yet. It will open your eyes to injustice and the inherent unfairness in institutional structures, identifying the times when you were oppressed and the times you were the oppressor. It will assemble all your judgy friends eagerly waiting to tell you their own opinions about your life choices. Though we sometimes ask our wisest friends for such counsel to help us with our life's direction, it's usually the trolls, or those most afraid of our becoming "different," who are quick to voice their disapproval. So, on this journey, how do we tune in to valuable advice and confidently reject the empty criticisms?

It's about both the substance of the remarks and the authenticity of the person giving their advice, right? Should I listen to someone calling me blasphemous when my spiritual journey doesn't fit neatly within my religious tradition's precepts and doctrines? Should I cast aside my feelings of awe and wonder when my rational friends insinuate that there's way too much woo-woo going on in my story? The changes that awakenings precipitate in us can raise truly dangerous questions about how we define our authentic selfhood, and about how and why we might choose to participate as we do in the world.

In Mary Oliver's poem "The Journey," she beautifully illustrates that the only life you can hear with utmost clarity—and therefore the only life you can save—is your own. In her poem, the external voices who clamor for you to "mend their life" must be considered background noise so that our own true self can emerge. And what most of those intentionally critical and dismissive questions tell us is that those who draw tight circles of who's in and who's out are threatened by anyone capable of drawing their circle wider. So, if you are broadening your circle in seemingly paradoxical ways, that really messes with people's sense of what they think they know. Have fun with that!

I have noticed that the more I wake up to my authentic self, the weirder I can seem to others, and though my circle of acceptance grows so much wider, my circle of those who seem to understand what I'm going through shrinks. Once you can get over being frightened of your own uniqueness, you'll discover it's quite freeing. My energy becomes focused on seeing the truth more clearly and loving more fully, and I care less about proving my point to those whose attention is on winning the argument du jour. Spiritual awakenings tend to bubble up from the gray zones, and they reside in the liminal places that refuse absolute certainty and scoff when mere correctness is the only thing drawn from them.

Yet we live in a consumerist cultural context that draws its energy from measurable success, well-defined answers, and a fixation on labeling others by their appropriate camp. So, if you aren't winning, you must be losing. If you're not right, then you are wrong. If you aren't a success, you are a failure. If you aren't in my ideological bubble, I may not even see you as human. Anything outside those boxes, anything that disrupts our assumption that this is now and always has been the way the world works seems suspect. Talking about the long-enduring wisdom that comes through love and truth, and answering questions with a lot more questions is a surefire way to get crucified—true a couple millennia ago or when your uncle who always has to be right comes over for family dinner.

Truth, as an ancient idea, is an aspect of wisdom that goes beyond mere statements of fact. It is a dynamic way of embracing paradoxical thinking that allows us to be constantly curious, in an unending search for meaning, in a context that asks the questions, "What else can I learn? How else can I grow?" We may feel pressed in our own time by the increasingly hostile polarities among people, but at some point, that has to break. In the eyes of God, claiming that humanity is limited to only the people who think my way, doesn't hold. God's circle is much more expansive than that. The Creator is in love with creation. The world is good. Human beings have always considered themselves a reflection of the gods, and so we too believe that the gods view justice and compassion in the best ways we can imagine as humans.

So, when those images get skewed—the world sucks, people suck, and love and justice are replaced with hate and brutality—we need to be reawakened to who God is and who we are, especially in relationship with one another. In such times of social unrest and personal wounding, that's when we are most likely to receive messages that it's time to wake up and notice what's true in the very, very long view of the world and be hopeful for the goodness of the existence of life once again.

In this time I believe we are ripe and ready for a renaissance of awakening that leads to transformation, the kind of transformation that aligns your inner moments of awe and wonder with your outer expressions of compassion and justice toward your neighbor. Transformation is an alignment of personal authenticity to be sure. But an awakening is fulfilled, not necessarily at the moment of transcendence, but as your internalization of it expresses benevolently in the world. True awakenings occur through a wide variety of experiences. And the spiritual transformation that comes from those experiences—though perhaps not as measurable or well-defined as the seven-step processes many transformation books sell—is nevertheless observable, truthful, life-giving, and hopeful.

In our current experience of major worldwide angst, I wonder: Will we be able to say, with Teresa of Ávila, "Let nothing disturb you"? Will we evoke Julian of Norwich, saying, "All shall be well," without a hint of sarcasm? Is it possible to understand the goodness of the world as they did? Is it possible to love not only our friends but also neighbors, strangers, and enemies?

Neither of these wise and passionate women were columnists in the Chicken Soup for the Soul genre, selling sentimental spirituality as a cure-all broth. Rather, they were addressing their own terrible times of being human, and they were doing it with a spiritual fortitude that's important to understand in our own time. They too lived through plague and war. They observed corruption in the church, and they had to choose their words carefully as women who were sharing their ideas with men holding all the ecclesial power. Their unwavering trust in God's grace to be enough and for God's ultimate plan to be soaked in goodness is not new, but it is certainly what we need right now.

Transformation Is Observable—It Is Not Hidden

To have such a comeback of spiritual awakening would be to offer a reset not just on humankind but on human kindness. I like to imagine this plethora of awakening moments being offered as the remedial curricula for being human. Whether these connections with spirit come through intense moments of curiosity, awe, and wonder, or the repeated practices of listening, sorting out, and processing divine truth, they reveal to us what it means to ponder the gift of life itself.

When all is well, when all is possible, when we feel our basic needs are met, we wake up to the need for compassion, justice, righteousness, hope, surrender, and mercy for the sake of all others. These three spiritually juicy words, "All is well," represent the fullness of divine grace bestowed on humanity and affirm the goodness of creation, which every major religion articulates in their own way. We, however, don't always come to accept such awakenings easily. They challenge our perceptions about God and about ourselves because they are meant to. It takes patience and hard work to stay awake and allow our insights to integrate into our own expressions of spiritual transformation. And it takes courage to begin again—and again—and again.

We are babies, all of us, in the ways of spiritual maturity. Reflecting on the spiritual life, yours or others, it is paradoxically true that the more you know, the more you realize how little you know. If you want to observe capable spiritual practitioners, well-versed in awakening, seek out those who are comfortable with being told they have a beginner's mind or a growth mindset. Flexibility is a spiritual virtue, although you may rarely hear that touted in faith communities. Hone that skill for your own sacred journey. Keep returning to curiosity, expand your consciousness through walks in nature or with a meditative practice—or by trying the entheogen route if you have a calling and a connection to vetted practitioners from the medical, psychological, or religious realms who will take your physical, emotional, and spiritual health seriously in preparing you for your journey. Commit to the quest that's on your heart. Practice the religion that your ancestors taught you. Become a prophet, a mystic, an activist, an artist, a contemplative, or just a human on the journey of seeking something more. All these paths show up again and again whenever someone is genuinely engaging the spiritual journey.

The paths are well trod. You don't go it alone. What I've learned from ancient texts, interesting classes, and lively conversations, I'm sharing here. It's my spin on millennia-old topics. The spiritual life is not hidden among ancient texts or esoteric practices; it's right here for you and for me to read about and try for ourselves.

Those who incorporate their awakenings into their lives will not only be flexible, they will also be different. Therein lies the "Oh, shit" moment on the road to spiritual awakenings. Humans tend to value stasis more than change. Those who become awakened and self-assured without needing to be right are weird. They will wander the dark and potentially lonely path.

There's a significant chance that the preservers of codified institutional religion will try to silence you. Remember that those who have spoken from a place of spiritual enlightenment have frequently faced criticism coming from within their own traditions. Transformative spiritual leaders have been oppressed and brutalized by those seeking to preserve religious purity. Take

Jesus's own ongoing confrontation with the scribes and Pharisees while he himself was a rabbinical teacher in the Judaism of his own time. I think about powerful leaders I have met, like the Rev. Janie Spahr, one of the first out "lesbyterians" in my tradition who faced verbal abuse and harassment but eventually saw the change she had advocated so hard for: ordination and marriage rights for LGBTQ+ clergy. I think about the young survivors of shootings in their schools who are now putting themselves in a brutal public arena calling for changes in gun laws. You might already know the leader of a movement that values the humanity of marginalized communities or a deeply mystical spiritual truth-teller who affirms the goodness of all creation. Ask them about their challenges and you may find the same story.

One of the reasons that faith-based communities are seeing significantly reduced commitments is that those who are waking up are simply walking away. They cannot abide the religious insiders who crack down on preserving the purity of institutional ways of being. They are frustrated that communities of faith aren't supporting the whole messy and tangled actual lives of people. Rather than allow the fresh air of spiritual innovation to propose what could be, old-timers are trying to preserve what was—when the sanctuaries and fellowship halls were full. And it doesn't matter one lick if the new ideas are in exact alignment with their sacred books' teachings on the spiritual life. When communities become traditional institutions, it's often not a spiritual life that's being encouraged, but a successful strategy for staying in business. Sadly, the creation of community life is drowned by legalism and doctrinal ass-puckering that strangle the living, breathing aspects of church life out of existence.

When the sacred meaning of the Julians and Teresas of the world is not met by religious community, then it's time to close the sanctuary doors and step outside for some air.

Whenever I hear someone say they are "spiritual but not religious," I hear them connecting with this broader feeling of unease or dismissal by the traditions of their upbringings. Believe me, it's way easier to bow out of the system than to stick with it and fight for its transformation. I know. That's why discerning what calling you have been awakened to and for is important. Many who wander the spiritual path find themselves wrestling with that decision: to lose touch with their home-base religion or confront the bullies who hold their beloved tradition captive to the stuckness of self-preservation.

When Jesus says about himself that the "Son of Man has nowhere to lay his head" (Matt 8:20; Luke 9:58), I take this to mean that those who are awakening will likely be spiritual nomads too. Following the way of Jesus, which is a way of transformation, carries a cost. Don't expect to find cozy companions in traditional communities of faith. You might be pleasantly surprised, but don't be blindsided if your powerful awakening story is met with confrontation or rejection. It may take some time to find your true people.

Those who are transformed will be open in both heart and mind. They will be curious about anything and everything. They will love deeply, even when they encounter strangers and tangle with enemies—and they will seek the truth, even when it challenges their own strongly held beliefs. They will be responsive and attentive to the needs of others. They will be different, perhaps even to the point of being troubled by the powers within their tradition. Maybe they'll be dismissed or ridiculed by those who use their tradition as a tool for power. The awakened and changed will be nomadic and a bit wild—seeking companions in all parts of their journey.

There's no getting ahead here, no diet that will be the right reset, no essential oils that will cure diseases. No snake oil, just humble servants seeking something much larger—seeking the spiritual life in a primal way, seeing life as beautiful. Understanding life is hard.

Knowing the characteristics that show up in transformed people is important, not for judging others, but for understanding your own benchmarks on the journey. You never quite know how far someone else has come or how far they have left to go. Comparison is the thief of joy, after all. But recall your spiritual companions across time like Teresa of Ávila, who, in her *Interior Castle*, provided a good assessment tool for the stages of spiritual development, a guide to use vigorously with yourself, and as kindly and gently as possible with others. In the words of our contemporary Glennon Doyle, queer activist and memoirist of her own transformation, "Be brave, you are a child of God. Be kind, everyone else is too!"

Transformation Is Truthful—It Does Not Lie

There is a painful truth about people, one that you will have to reckon with the more you allow yourself to tread the path toward spiritual transformation: human beings are all—and I mean *all*—sacred, holy, and beloved.

Sure, there is good and evil in this world. We experience both every day. Yet calling someone a saint or a sinner only describes a part of who they are. It is never the whole package. If the souls and spirit of people really matter, and the world is indeed created good, why do so many—and I mean so, so many—people suck? Presuming that God is love and that all life is valuable to God puts in our face this idea of the sacredness of every member of humanity.

Spiritual transformation is possible when such foundational truths are awakened and fully embraced—truths frequently taught by faith practitioners all around the globe from a variety of traditions. (Refresher: Love God. Love one another. And I like to add my summary of most religions' moral mandates: Don't be an asshole.) These principled values are also sometimes thought to be inalienable simply from a humanist perspective. Valuing life and practicing loving-kindness seems to work for our species—a lot of the time.

Yet living through an age when truth seems to be a relative concept and the brute force of individualism claims self-preservation as its highest value, we are flabbergasted that people believe propaganda and conspiracy theories that seems patently crazy and ridiculous. Perhaps truth in this manifestation is a lost value, a guidepost that no longer makes sense, as reality seems to be whatever is coming through everyone's own filtered lens. But capital-T Truth still follows ancient guidelines and cannot so easily be dismissed by the power of rhetoric or playing on people's underlying beliefs or fears. Spiritual Truth remains consistent, giving it the power to be a factor for transformation.

Truth in the sacred realm holds a kind of perennial authority. But it's rather hard to put into words. It isn't a mere assertion of facts, that's clear. It cannot be eroded by gossip or tainted by outright lies. It is always noted as one of the pillars of religious understanding, and it is why awakening experiences leave us with the sense of the "really real," as though the rest of life were more like a rehearsal and the awakening itself was the true reality. I wish I could put it into a theological system or make it make sense here. The poets and mystics help: poetry, prayer, and the contributions of artists and musicians put our angst into conversation with the beauty of the world. In our broken and hurting world, such love and connection with one another and with our sacred source will always have an aspirational quality to it. We can only get better at it. We can never achieve perfect Love or perfect Truth; nevertheless, when we are awakened, we can't unsee those ideals. They become our ultimate goals for living a transformed life.

The spiritually awake person also lives with the painful reality that they can't fall back asleep. You can't go back to being the way you were prior to the aha moment that set you on your own unique path. Once you move out of self-preservation mode and into a sense that all life is sacred and the world is good, then the other things you perhaps thought of as important in life suddenly are rendered less than. You don't need to be rich, popular, or famous. You don't even need to be liked. All else is vanity. All else is rubbish. All else ceases to make sense. Yes, you still need food, shelter, and the basics of life, yet opening up to Truth puts even the sustenance of your own existence into perspective.

Look back on your life story, either from your connection with previous chapters or from a chapter in your experience only you can describe, when Truth became real for you, when you embraced beauty. How about Love? Understanding? Compassion? When did you notice a lifting of the veil connecting you directly to the source of divine love? Even when you can't fully explain to another person the details or the why of your awakening, you recognized the truth when you experienced it. And maybe then you kept seeing that truth everywhere. Even in the quest for scientific understanding of our world, the patterns and purpose of life in all its diversity seem to sing with the goodness of creation.

Lies and the liars who tell them will be terrified of such bold and beautiful insights. They will seek to dismiss the Truth as weak or stupid, and they will fill any void with faulty or useless information. Reader, friend, fake news around every corner is exhausting. But there is nothing new under the sun. Truth is ancient, sure. But lies are too, from the very beginning. "False witness" shows up in the Ten Commandments as a "Thou shalt not bear it." The desire to cover up reality and bend it to our control is pretty damn old. The vanity that the teacher talks about in the book of Ecclesiastes sounds like it could have been written yesterday. Life is repetitive, boring, and short—and *nevertheless* precious to us even in all its mess and disillusionment.

You take the good. You take the bad. You take them both and there you have ... *yes,* you have *The Facts of Life* theme song running through your head. (Thank you, catchy 1980s television jingle writer Gloria Loring.) But the song goes on to say that when the world never seems to be living up to your dreams, suddenly you're finding out the facts of life are all about you. The facts, as Job discovered them on his biblical ash heap after everything he loved had been lost, remind us that the world seems to give and to take away. It feels enormously unfair. Yet to assert that the good we experience in this life is all reward and the bad is all punishment is a false narrative.

Transformation—that beginning again and again and again—ultimately takes us on this journey of highs and lows. Seeing the world with eyes wide open will show you amazing goodness and beauty. It will also show you cruelty and heartache. Truth as a spiritual virtue isn't about being able to make the world function with all justice, righteousness, and love, but about pointing out with clarity whenever a commitment to truth has been lost, when justice is absent, or righteousness is overturned, or love is replaced by hate.

War will always include civilian casualties, especially among those who have no power or means to save themselves. Will corporations still find ways to approach slave labor in their practices? Yes. Will countries still go to war for legitimate and terrible reasons? Yes.

The world remains good. People remain worth saving. All shall be well; that's the mantra for the spiritual life—even when it's far from well and hugely disturbing, even when some take advantage of others. That's the time when awakened folks are needed the most. Awakening is a beginning again.

Transformation Is Life-Giving—And Life Is Messy

The mystics seem to say these very mundane things that, when you're given space to think about them, sound either ridiculously naive or utterly profound: "All shall be well." "Let nothing disturb you. Let nothing upset you.

Everything changes. God alone is unchanging." You're tempted to ask, have you peeked in on the shitshow lately? It's not looking good out there.

I sometimes want to ask the visionaries of other time periods if they felt brave or crazy or a little of both as they eschewed getting worked up about the despairs and depravities of their own times. Just fuhgeddaboudit—in my best New Jersey accent—seems to be what they are saying. Don't worry. Atrocities of the world? They come and go. They aren't what matters. And what kind of world were they living in? Plagues? Check. Wars? Check. Greedy elites? Check. Fear and foreboding about the future? Check and check.

The visionaries weren't part of some wonderful utopian dream of "life is good" T-shirts. They were counseling real people with real problems. They were looking to God to make sense of the senselessness within their own times and places. They understood that life would continue to be messy. The wellness that Julian of Norwich promises is not that everything will be perfect in your own life, but as a whole, your life will be yours, a gift, a wellness to be treasured no matter what happens. Teresa of Ávila, in the "Let nothing disturb you" quote she kept with her as a bookmark, reminds us that God alone is enough. Not magic. Not a guarantee of wealth or status or fame. God is enough. Enough for us to begin to see the goodness in the world, no matter what is swirling all around us.

Today I see so much despair, especially as our youngest generations take note of the great troubles of our globalized and interdependent twenty-first-century world. There was a time when nations and peoples who didn't get along could count on the relative independence of being long-distance neighbors. But what happens around the globe now affects us, and every kind of social and political system is interconnected through economic ups and downs, if nothing else.

Youthful seers and visionaries are rightly concerned about the state of the world and want to see and make changes to ensure the thriving of our species on this planet, which is a pressure cooker of overcrowding and climate change. Should they call bullshit on their living elders' stale ideas for fixing a world they created but can no longer protect? Absolutely. Should they dismiss any hope whatsoever that people can change or even will want to embrace change? I feel their pain and exhaustion looking at a sketchy present and sketchier future, but I hope they will find their footing and keep pressing for change. I want them to cling to knowing that the world is being held by something bigger that we can only glimpse in visions. I want them to know that even amid the pain of this world, God is enough. I want them to know that in the much larger, much longer trajectory of this planetary existence, truly, "All shall be well."

Life as we experience it is messy and hard. Some days it feels as though the experiment of creation isn't worth the trouble. But, my friends, it surely is. Being transformed means seeing the power of these visions supporting life in the present moment, and in the eternal now, as you say or try to say these words that catch in your throat: All shall be well. God is enough. You are alive. Remember that it is worth giving our attention to what life is calling us to be.

There are no quick fixes or twelve-step programs, only doing the next right thing, only putting one foot in front of the other. And that's okay. The spiritual journey always begins right now, in the present.

Transformation Is Hopeful— It Is Renewed Every Morning

Mystics, prophets, artists, poets, and spiritual practitioners of every kind have a couple of things in common: They are radical realists, and they are fiercely hopeful. I was fortunate to learn about this combo from my theology mentor in seminary, Dr. Douglas Ottati. His book *Hopeful Realism: The Poetry of Theology* captures with brevity the theological message I hope this book conveys in spirituality. As theology focuses on concepts about who God is, spirituality is the practice of encountering and knowing who God is. For both endeavors, a hopeful realism is necessary.

To live in the messy, difficult real world, it's hard to hold that radical realism and fierce hope. You quickly learn there is no perfect plan for happiness. You might respond with avoidance and despair, drowning yourself with numbing behaviors—filling the space with activities or addictions. You might blame everyone else but your in-group. But being both real and hopeful is something that will stretch you spiritually.

Awakenings also tend to hold both qualities: they boldly give us a picture of what's really real—good or bad, wonderful or terrifying. And then they have a luminous, visionary quality that allows us to hold hope for ourselves and perhaps even our world. True awakenings are inspirational, and purposeful, and they direct the steps of our lives—if we let go of our fears and let them lead us. We become followers long before any of us comes to grips with being leaders in any spiritual sense.

This hope can be painful, because you start to see what could be, what should be, but what isn't yet in our world. Not gonna lie: Reality can be the worst—waking up to how nightmarish the world really is. The spiritual visionaries who look that reality in the eye are therefore truth tellers of the oddest sort. They cut right to the actuality and point to what could be different—better.

One of the biblical visionary truth tellers was Mary. In the glory of her song, the Magnificat (Luke 1:46–55), she samples and builds on an ancestor song from Hannah (1 Sam 2:1–10), reminding us of the mystics who carry the weight of the world in their hearts. Both of these biblical women, who tell us straight up that their souls magnify and amplify the very nature of God, articulate a vision where the lowly are lifted up and valued and the mighty are brought down from their thrones, where there is a not-so-casual reversal of how the world seems to work against the marginalized. That's radical, real, and hopeful. It is the transformed spirit, fully awake, fully engaged in putting words into action.

Hopeful realism results from transformation and curiosity, the acceptance of the quest, learning the patterns of religious truth, deconstructing the bullshit of religious facades, acceptance of what is, letting go of what no longer serves you or your neighbor, and leaning into the hope of the callings and consolations of your life's journey. This transformation begins with us, as we allow ourselves to change. Being changed ourselves, we become free to be agents of meaningful change in the systems and institutions of our world. We need people who are awake to the reality *and* hopeful for the future as religion, education, government, health care, and every facet of our human life in community is shaped for community. The bliss may not be something you can hang on to, but it will fuel you as you take your next steps.

Begin Again

Yes, it's been said before. Spiritual awakening requires response. We all keep starting over and over again. Beginner's mind. The growth mindset. Pandora's box. Eating the mushroom. Taking that pilgrimage. Waking up. The next step. Even so, just when we think we have it all figured out, there will be something new to learn about ourselves or others.

I've written this book as I myself have yearned for the validation of knowing that these awakening experiences are both common among the human species and uniquely wonderful for the individuals who experience them. I've understood that to experience all these things isn't a sign of specialness—it's not—but a sign of our shared humanity and our incredible range for spiritual exploration.

There are no experts in this realm, really. There are people who simply awaken and respond and keep responding in radical hope and realism. This book isn't about doing spirituality perfectly, but about listening, seeing, and interpreting what we experience and see and how we move our quest and calling forward. That's it. We listen to the inner voice; we listen to the stories of others. We see reality for what it knows and for what we hope it could be. And we seek to make sense of what we learn so that we can apply that knowledge to our own choices and behaviors.

I'm no great expert on spiritual wonders. You may not be either. But we can experience awakenings and observe human life, and think about what it means to be this particular kind of spiritually tuned-in creature.

Maybe I did fulfill my childhood fantasy of being like Jane Goodall, except I turned my study toward my inner primate rather than carefully observing the ones in the jungle. Something wonderful happens when you trust the spiritual life to be real and start to recognize your own awakenings as the longing for and realization of human transformation.

I hope and pray that, having read this book, you will find the confidence you need to live into your own spiritual strengths. As you do, you will be drawn into paradoxical thinking. You will recognize your own worldview as a gift and, simultaneously, be fascinated by the worldviews of others. You will be curious about your own place in the world and attentive to the direction your own life is taking. You will cultivate a deeper sense of compassion—possibly even for your enemies and persecutors, those whom Jesus described in his Sermon on the Mount. This transformation will set you apart, bring you into a humble sense of your shared humanity, and start you wondering.

May you continue to hunger for and be satisfied by your own ongoing true awakening!

TIME TO WAKE UP

Time to stay awake.

Not that you won't need rest for the journey. You will, and it's okay to pause and breathe anytime you need to. Sleep is important in knowing the Spirit, for the dreaming is as valuable as the doing when it comes to understanding your inner voice.

But if you are open to it, you will keep on awakening, wave after wave after wave.

That's the spiritual transformation, the one you've earned by traversing all those highs and lows, by untangling the mess of your life or simply letting the mess be a part of your life.

Where will you begin again?

Is some unexplored spiritual terrain beckoning you to give it a whirl?

Is there familiar ground calling you back to go deeper?

Keep on making the path by walking. Keep on engaging the Source of life itself and you won't stay bored for long.

And bring a friend or two along as a traveling companion—whether it's someone who is living and breathing in this time and you can go it together, or whether it's consulting with some old friends like Teresa and Julian who've worn the path before you.

"All shall be well, and all shall be well, and all manner of things shall be well."

Let nothing disturb you. Let nothing upset you. Everything changes. God alone is unchanging. With patience all things are possible. Whoever has God lacks nothing. God alone is enough.

SOURCES

Chapter 1

Becker, Jane. 2023. *Ted Lasso*. Season 3, episode 10. Producers: J. Lawrence, B. Sudeikis, B. Hunt, and J. Kelly. Apple TV.

Brown, Brené. 2010. "The Power of Vulnerability." TED.com. https://www.ted.com/talks/brene_brown_the_power_of_vulnerability.

Campbell, Joseph. 1991. *Reflections on the Art of Living: A Joseph Campbell Companion*. Edited by D. K. Obson. HarperCollins.

Keys, Donald. 1982. *Earth at Omega: Passage to Planetization*. Branden Press.

Smith, Huston. 2000. *Cleansing the Doors of Perception: The Religious Significance of Entheogenic Plants and Chemicals*. Tarcher Putnam.

Teresa of Ávila. 2003. *The Interior Castle*. Translated by Mirabai Starr. Riverhead Books.

Chapter 2

Calvin, John. 1960. *Calvin: Institutes of the Christian Religion*. 2 volumes. Volume 1. Edited by John T. McNeill. Translated by Ford Lewis Battles. Library of Christian Classics 20. Westminster Press.

Doyle, Glennon. n.d. Twitter. https://twitter.com/glennondoyle/status.

Einstein, Albert. 1955 (May 2). "Old Man's Advice to Youth: 'Never Lose a Holy Curiosity.'" *LIFE*, 64.

Julian of Norwich. 1373/1998. *Revelations of Divine Love*. Translated by E. Spearing. Penguin Classics.

Palmer, Albert W. 1911. *The Mountain Trail and Its Message*. Pilgrim Press.

Teresa of Ávila. 2019. *The Collected Works of St. Teresa of Ávila*. Vol. 1. ICS Publications.

Chapter 3

Finley, James. 2024 (July). "Interior Castle Online Course." Center for Action and Contemplation.

Teresa of Ávila. 2003. *The Interior Castle*. Translated by Mirabai Starr. Riverhead Books.

Tolkien, J. R. R. 1954/2004. *The Fellowship of the Ring*. Houghton Mifflin.

Chapter 4

Brown, Brené. 2010. *The Gift of Imperfection: Let Go of Who You Think You're Supposed to Be and Embrace Who You Are*. Hazelden.

L'Engle, Madeleine. 1973. *A Wind in the Door*. Farrar, Straus and Giroux.

Taylor, Barbara Brown. 2019. *Holy Envy: Finding God in the Faith of Others*. HarperCollins.

Chapter 5

Fox, Ruth Marlene. "Four-Fold Benedictine Blessing." As quoted in https://www.thesacredbraid.com/2016/07/22/a-non-traditional-blessing/.

Prince and the Revolution. 1984. "Let's Get Crazy." *Purple Rain*. Warner Bros.

R.E.M. 1991. "Losing My Religion." *Out of Time*. Comp. B. Berry, P. Buck, M. Mills, and M. Stipe. Warner Bros.

Tickle, Phyllis. 2008. *The Great Emergence: How Christianity Is Changing and Why*. Baker Books.

Chapter 6

Anonymous. [14th century] / 1922. *The Cloud of Unknowing*. Edited by Evelyn Underhill. John M. Watkins.

Finley, James. 2023, September 4. "Turning to the Mystics: Turning to Mechthild of Magdeburg." Podcast. Center for Action and Contemplation.

Julian of Norwich. 1373/1998. *Revelations of Divine Love*. Translated by E. Spearing. Penguin Classics.

Rumi, Jalaluddin. 2004. *Rumi: Selected Poems*. Translated by Coleman Barks with John Moyne. Penguin Books.

Teresa of Ávila. 2003. *The Interior Castle*. Translated by Mirabai Starr. Riverhead Books.

Chapter 7

Armstrong, Louis. 1967. "What a Wonderful World." Comp. Bob Thiele and George David Weiss. *What a Wonderful World*. George David. Performed by Armstrong, Louis. 1967. "What A Wonderful World." ABC Records.

"Discernment." n.d. Ligare: A Christian Psychedelic Society. https://www.ligare.org/beforeyoutry#. Adapted and used by permission.

Jung, Carl. n.d. "Carl Jung: I Don't Need to Believe. I Know." YouTube. https://youtu.be/kb0toLBlofE?si=RbghCOoFgrNM1h6a.

Mande, Joe, and Chris Encell. 2019, January 17. "Chidi Sees the Time Knife." *The Good Place*. Season 3, episode 12. NBC.

Scharper, Julie. 2017. "Crash Course in the Nature of Mind." *Johns Hopkins Magazine*. https://hub.jhu.edu/magazine/2017/fall/roland-griffiths-magic-mushrooms-experiment-psilocybin-depression/.

Chapter 8

Brumm, Joe. 2024. "The Sign." Bluey Wiki. https://blueypedia.fandom.com/wiki/The_Sign.

Campbell, Joseph. 1991. *Reflections on the Art of Living: A Joseph Campbell Companion*. Edited by D. K. Obson. HarperCollins.

Levoy, Gregg. 1997. *Callings: Finding and Following an Authentic Life*. Three Rivers Press.

Oliver, Mary. 1992. *New and Selected Poems*. Volume 1. Beacon Press.

Chapter 9

Palmer, Parker J. 2000. *Let Your Life Speak: Listening for the Voice of Vocation*. Jossey-Bass.

Baxter, Richard. 1656/1974. *The Reformed Pastor.* Banner of Truth Trust.

Clements, Ron, and John Musker. 1992. *Aladdin.* Buena Vista Pictures.

Chapter 10

Calvin, John. 1960. *Calvin: Institutes of the Christian Religion.* 2 volumes. Volume 1. Edited by John T. McNeill. Translated by Ford Lewis Battles. Library of Christian Classics 20. Westminster Press.

Doyle, Glennon. n.d. Twitter. https://twitter.com/glennondoyle/status.

Julian of Norwich. 1373/1998. *Revelations of Divine Love.* Translated by E. Spearing. Penguin Classics.

Loring, Gloria. 1984. "The Facts of Life." *A Shot in the Dark.* Glitz Records.

Ottati, Douglas F. 1999. *Hopeful Realism: Reclaiming the Poetry of Theology.* Pilgrim Press.

"Rev. Dr. Jane Adams Spahr." n.d. LGBTQ Religious Archives. https://lgbtqreligiousarchives.org/profiles/jane-adams-spahr.

Teresa of Ávila. 2019. *The Collected Works of St. Teresa of Ávila.* Vol. 1. ICS Publications.

ACKNOWLEDGMENTS

I would like to thank my husband Chuck for the permission to share our family's awakening moments as a real-world example of the highs, the lows, and the mess of life itself. I am grateful to my children, Cade and Ryleigh for their ongoing curiosity, determined kindness, and never-ending ability to keep this spiritual spokesperson's feet firmly on the ground. I am grateful to the many teachers whose lessons infiltrate this book, some named, some unnamed, some living, some I've only known from the words they put on a page in their own times. I wrote this book upon the ideas and insights of many who have experienced awakenings of their own! Thanks to all my friends who read sections of this book pre-publication—providing helpful feedback and the encouragement to keep writing. I also want to thank the Ligare community for continuing to make connections at the intersection of Christianity/Spirituality and psychedelics. This book has come into being because of spiritual nudges answered through that group of friends. And finally, thanks to my editor, Lillian Copan, who was paying attention to where the Spirit was showing up and took a chance that there would be insights in this book that would be valuable to reveal. Her commitment to working alongside me to find the words for some rather indescribable kinds of mysteries has made this book so much better.